Trusting GOD When You're STRUGGLING
Overcoming Obstacles to
FAITH

C.E. WHITE

Trusting God When You're Struggling:
Overcoming Obstacles to Faith by C.E. White
Copyright © 2020 by Connie E. White

All rights reserved. This book or any portion thereof may not be reproduced or used in any manner whatsoever without the express written permission of the publisher except for the use of brief quotations in a book review.

Scripture quotations, unless otherwise indicated in the footnotes, are from the ESV® Bible (The Holy Bible, English Standard Version®), copyright © 2001 by Crossway, a publishing ministry of Good News Publishers. Used by permission. All rights reserved.

Italics added in Scripture are the author's emphasis.

Printed in the United States of America
ISBN: 978-1-7332487-2-3

cewhitebooks@gmail.com
www.cewhitebooks.com
www.instagram.com/cewhitebooks
www.facebook.com/cewhitebooks

First Edition, November 2020

Cover design by Jessica Bagge
Interior design by Kevin G. Summers

To my beloved friend and critique partner Sharon—your insight sharpened this book in its dull places, and your encouragement kept me writing through my own.

CONTENTS

Section One - Overcoming The Obstacles 1
Finding His Promise 3
Expectations 6
Fear 11
Self-Sufficiency 19
Doubt 27
Pleasure 34
Abandonment 42
Insufficiency 50
Failure 56
Suffering, Persecution, And Other Generally Hard Things 62
Distraction 75
Laziness 86
Hurry 95
Prosperity 106
Worry 115
Dreams 123
Conformity 132
Regret 143
The Cares Of This World 151
Section Two - Building Spiritual Health 157
Preventative Measures 159
Belief 163
Hope 171
Prayer 178
Fasting 188
Satisfaction 193
Thankfulness 201
Delight 208
Things Unseen 215

SECTION ONE
Overcoming the Obstacles

FINDING HIS PROMISE

The way of Jesus cannot be imposed or mapped—it requires an active participation in following Jesus as He leads us through sometimes strange and unfamiliar territory.

Eugene H. Peterson, *The Jesus Way*

When's the last time you felt unencumbered by the things of this world? Most of us probably have a tough time answering that. There's too much wrestling for our attention and shifting our eyes off God, but asking the question still gives me hope, because I know God's promise for us.

"Come to Me, and I will give you rest," He says.[1]

"Be anxious for nothing."[2]

I want to live in God's rest and in light of what I truly believe—that this world is not my home. I want to fix my eyes on Jesus. I want to pray without ceasing.[3] I want to walk away from the mirror of the Word and remember what I look like for more than a moment or two. In short, I want to be a doer, not just a hearer.[4] I want to live in the freedom Christ offers.

1 Matt 11:28
2 Phil 4:6
3 I Thess 5:16
4 James 1:22-25

So, what keeps me in chains, and how do I get out of them? I'm going to explore many of the things that keep us from trusting God when things are difficult. I want to do this not because I've mastered the art, but because I know the study will drive me deeper into His Word where the lessons and truths will establish themselves in my own heart.

Like the Israelites, God's salvation took me out of slavery, and I was grateful. But He's also led me into the desert, and it turns out I don't always like the desert. It's uncomfortable and boring and hard. I don't understand it, and I never feel settled. I'm starting to wonder where we're even going. I'm grumbling. I want comfort. I want pleasure and ease and accolades and security and control, and the desert gives little opportunity for such things. The only thing to rely on in the desert is God, and I'm too often not content to depend on His daily sustenance and bask in His presence.

Ouch. It hurts my heart to say those words, because deep down, I know *God is worth it*. I know what He has for me—what He has for all who are heavy laden—is good. It's rest. It's peace. It's love and freedom, and He's taking me to the Promised Land. But that doesn't mean it's always easy.

Receiving God's rest is also about giving up myself. I can't follow Him to the Promised Land (or anywhere else) if I'm still hanging on to my own agenda. And ultimately, hanging on to my agenda is a lack of trust. It means either I don't believe He knows what He's doing or that He's capable of doing it or that He really wants what's best for me.

Wasn't that the crime of the Israelites? A simple lack of faith that He was taking them where He said He would? A weariness with the monotony and wandering with no time frame, no understanding of His plan, and a waning hope in what was promised?

When I was young, I used to judge the Israelites for their lack of faith. How could they doubt God when they'd seen all the miracles He did in Egypt and throughout their own history?

Time tempered my arrogance as my own grumblings appeared. The temptation to follow my own path—one that makes sense and feels good—looms constantly in my mind, pounding my faith like a battering ram.

The only way to walk in the desert with joy is to trust God, and the only way to trust Him is to know Him. But if we're in the desert without all the things we think we want, what's the point? Why keep doing it? And what is this rest He offers? Can we get past all the obstacles to experience it?

God says we can, and I believe Him. Let's find out what it takes.

EXPECTATIONS

Expectations were like fine pottery. The harder you held them, the more likely they were to crack.

Brandon Sanderson, *The Way of Kings*

Expectations are a double-edged sword. They can be the beautiful hope as you await the fulfillment of God's promise, or they can be your biggest source of discontentment and disappointment. They are what you allow them to be. If you let go of the "what might have beens" and fix your eyes on the blessings God has in front of you instead, you will find that rest and peace He offers.

Our expectations often remain in the periphery until we start to think time is running out and they may never be realized. Then we pass some subconscious deadline, and they begin to fester into discontentment—

Maybe you don't become disillusioned with your singleness until you hit thirty and all your friends are married.

Maybe you don't get frustrated with your financial situation until you are still living paycheck-to-paycheck at forty.

Maybe you don't get angry over your failing health until you've lost the weight, taken the supplements, finished the treatment.

And then it strikes. God hasn't come through, and your circumstances are no longer "fair." Where is God now? Isn't this when He's supposed to show up? What will your response be if He doesn't?

Abraham and Sarah may be the best examples of how NOT to handle our expectations. God told Abram to uproot his entire life, and with that command came the promise that he would father a great nation.[5]

Abraham believed God and did as He asked. But as the years went on, the promise seemed more and more far-fetched. Seven years had passed when we see Abraham start to question: "But Abram said, 'O Lord God, what will you give me, for I continue childless, and the heir of my house is Eliezer of Damascus?' And Abram said, 'Behold, you have given me no offspring, and a member of my household will be my heir.'"

But God reassured him: "'This man shall not be your heir; your very own son shall be your heir.' And He brought him outside and said, 'Look toward heaven, and number the stars, if you are able to number them.' Then He said to him, 'So shall your offspring be.' And he believed the Lord, and He counted it to him as righteousness."[6]

We can relate, right? Abraham performed this drastic act of obedience, uprooting his entire life, family, and business. Can you imagine if your family suffered from infertility and God came to you saying, "Move to Africa right now. Leave everything you know, and I will give you a child?" What if seven years later you were still childless? I'd be questioning, too.

But with this reassurance, Abraham went on in faith. God took note. Abraham still believed; he just needed some encouragement. So far, so good.

Fast-forward four more years. No child. So they took matters into their own hands.

---

5   Genesis 12:1-3
6   Genesis 15:2-6

Maybe this is what God meant, they probably thought.

And we all know the story. Abraham fathered Ishmael with Sarah's handmaid and sparked an enmity and unrest that lasts into our own time.

The promised son Isaac was born fourteen years later—twenty-five long years after God's initial promise and well beyond the point of human possibility. The fulfillment was beautiful, but it was shadowed by the disbelief along the way.

What if they had waited for what God had in store?

How many times have you taken matters into your own hands? God didn't hand you the job, the relationship, the money. So, you scrambled. You grasped in desperation, trying to find a way to get what you want—*what He promised you.*

And eventually, you made it happen. You got a job in that field, but the leadership was toxic, and the work fell flat. You got married, but your spouse had a violent temper you never saw before the wedding. You bought those things you deserved with a credit card and ended up in a nightmare of debt.

Your Ishmaels. You thought they would satisfy you, but they just caused more strife, more disillusionment, more heartache.

But what if you had waited?

What if the promise is twenty-five years in coming? Can you walk in the desert that long without succumbing to your human wiles to get what you want?

If you really believe there is an Isaac coming—if you *really* trust God—you can.

But more often than I'd like to admit, we stop believing sometime in those dry years. We misunderstood. God doesn't care. He wants us to act.

God helps those who help themselves, we think.

But that's just what we say when we stop believing He wants to help us at all.

I have learned that when I feel that desperation urging me to claw and push and do whatever it takes to attain something, it is never of the Lord. Because that desperation is fear, and fear is never from Him. "There is no fear in love, but perfect love casts out fear. For fear has to do with punishment, and whoever fears has not been perfected in love."[7]

If you feel that fearful grasping and are on the verge of taking matters into your own hands, take a step back. Look at Abraham and Sarah and see the beauty of the Lord's fulfillment of their dreams vs. the strife of their own attempt.

I find solace in the fact that despite Abraham and Sarah's doubts, they are still commended for their faith in Hebrews 11, the "Faith Chapter." "By faith, Abraham, when called to go to a place he would later receive as his inheritance, obeyed and went, even though he did not know where he was going. By faith, he made his home in the Promised Land like a stranger in a foreign country; he lived in tents, as did Isaac and Jacob, who were heirs with him of the same promise. For he was looking forward to the city with foundations, whose architect and builder is God. And by faith even Sarah, who was past childbearing age, was enabled to bear children because she considered Him faithful who had made the promise. And so from this one man, and he as good as dead, came descendants as numerous as the stars in the sky and as countless as the sand on the seashore."[8]

Though their faith faltered and their journey was imperfect, God still ultimately counted them among the faithful. So when you look back at your own "Ishmael" in shame, remember it is not the end of your story. "The steadfast love of the Lord nev-

---

[7] 1 John 4:18
[8] Hebrews 11:8-12

er ceases; His mercies never come to an end; they are new every morning; great is Your faithfulness."[9]

His mercies are new every morning, so your chance to trust Him starts fresh every day. The fulfillment of God's promise will always be glorious. And how much more beautiful is that fulfillment when all hope seems lost?

TAKEAWAYS:

- God has His own timeline, but He will always keep His word. Hold fast to Him.
- Expectation is not the enemy, but when you place your hope in circumstances and personal desires instead of on God Himself, you will lose your direction.
- The fulfillment of God's promise is not dependent on your perfect faith. Abraham and Sarah doubted along the way but always came back to their belief in God's character. "I believe; help my unbelief!"[10] is a perfectly acceptable response to God!
- God's promise is no less sweet when it comes later than you thought possible. Indeed, joy is often the most profound when the blessing is, by all accounts, impossible and anyone sensible would have given up.

---

9 Lamentations 3:22-23
10 Matthew 9:24

FEAR

David didn't kill Goliath because he set out to slay giants...he killed Goliath because his dad sent him to take his brothers sandwiches, and Goliath got in the way.

Rich Mullins

Fear is a liar. It's a master of disguise, a viral contagion, an iceberg hidden beneath the surface just waiting to wreck you. Fear told me I didn't have what it takes to write this chapter. I kept flitting away from the page and finding excuses not to begin. Snacks may have been involved.

I'll just scroll the internet, I thought. *No one knows I'm writing this anyway, and nobody will care. Who am I? Someone else can do it better.*

Fear doesn't want me to take a risk and put myself out there. Stepping out is dangerous; I might get hurt. Better just live a quiet life and keep to myself. Fear is a bully that will taunt, blame, accuse, and belittle just to keep you from taking a chance and failing...or succeeding. It would rather you stay on the sidelines than get into the game, and its tactics are relentless.

It would be easy to stop there—to say all you have to do is stand up to the bully, and he will go away. More often than not, that would be true. Ninety-five percent of the things you fear will never happen, and you can't control the rest.

OK, I just made those numbers up, but you get the idea.

However, sometimes fear speaks the truth. There's a real threat, a real enemy.

Sometimes, you really don't have what it takes.

Sometimes, cancer is bigger than the doctors.

Sometimes, fear is a giant—a Goliath.

What then?

Every day for forty days, Goliath came out to insult and mock the Israelites. Every day, they cowered at the sight of this giant decked out in his finest armor.

Until David showed up. This giant inciting terror into the armies of the living God was an affront to everything David knew of the Lord, and he wanted to stand up to it.

His brothers said he was arrogant and negligent.

The king said he was untrained.

This is often the reaction when you step out in faith. Others don't understand. They're either jealous, ashamed, or fearful themselves. But David would not be turned aside.

So they tried to give him the tools that made sense—armor, a helmet, a sword—but David knew his weapon was the Lord. He already understood that "some trust in chariots and some in horses, but we trust in the name of the Lord our God," as he would later write in the Psalms.[11]

You know the story. Seemingly against all odds, David won. And he did so using the humble tools God had put in his life along the way. Trust that God is preparing you to face the battles He has before you. You don't need a mighty weapon. You only need Him on your side.

11   Psalm 20:7

But let's go back a little further, because *David's battle against fear didn't start with Goliath.*

He tells Saul about killing a lion and a bear to defend his flock, and he gives God credit for those victories. I'm guessing he was pretty frightened when facing down the teeth and claws of those deadly predators. Maybe he wasn't totally confident in his ability to defeat them, but he stood strong because it was the duty God had given him, and he wanted to do it well. I'm going to go further back and bet that David's confidence in God was proven even before the lion or the bear. Maybe it started the first night he had to sleep under the open sky alone with the sheep.

The key is that during his moments of fear, David turned to the Lord. Even in his daily life, he knew God was the one defending him, and he stepped out beyond his own strength because he trusted. Trusting along the way gave him the strength to step out before Goliath.

Fear keeps many of us in bondage every day. You want to reach out to that person, but they might think you're strange. You want to write that book (ahem), but what if it's a flop? You want to apply for that job, but you know you're underqualified.

But if you never walk out past your own abilities, how will you ever believe God has your back? What will happen when your Goliath comes along?

You will probably cower in terror like the Israelites because Goliath is too much for you. You never gave God the chance to be big in your life. You kept Him small by not taking risks, by not stepping out in faith, by not fighting the battles in front of you.

If you don't start fighting the lion today, you'll never be able to fight Goliath when he shows up. The lion, at least, had no malice; the attack wasn't personal. It was just a threat common to all men. But your Goliath is coming after you every day shouting:

You're worthless. You're weak. You're a fool. You can't do it. God doesn't care. God isn't strong enough.

And even when Goliath isn't shouting, his presence is enough to remind you. He's standing across the field, imposing and confident, armed with every tool the world has to offer, making you more and more aware of your inadequacy.

What is your Goliath? Fear has a thousand faces, and most of us could pick any one out of an embarrassingly long list, but for this exercise, just pick one—the one that's crushing your soul and keeping you in bondage. It doesn't have to be a physical fear; it can be an emotional threat or a mental one.

What would it take for you to defeat that fear? Does it seem impossible? Risky? Nuts? Does the idea of fighting make you want to cower beneath your covers? All those things probably applied to David fighting Goliath. Yet, he trusted God to see him through it. Do you? Can you step out beyond your fear into the unknown where there is real danger? Can you trust that the tools He's given you along the way are all you need to defeat the giant?

I guarantee Goliath is too big for you. He's too big for the best armor and the strongest sword, and all your knowledge and common sense. But He's not too big for the Lord.

You may be thinking, "I thought this chapter was supposed to be making me feel safe!" And it is, but not in yourself. *The best-laid plans of mice and men*[12]…as they say. But God is not a mouse or a man, and His plans, while often scary, are always the best. Our own plans, no matter how good and sensible, tend to go awry or leave us feeling unfulfilled and listless.

Taking the safe road is rarely a road to actual safety. More often, it is a path of false security keeping you from the freedom of relying on the Lord, keeping your life stagnant and empty, and

---

12   From the poem "To a Mouse" by Robert Burns

keeping you from stepping out so that you can learn He's trustworthy. It's keeping you from helping people, from reaching your potential, from living a full life. Giving in to fear is cowing to everything bad that could possibly happen—most of which never will. It's living your life at the mercy of whatever negative possibility creeps into your mind. And that's not living at all.

The safe road urges us to do the sensible thing—to trust in our horses and chariots (or our 401ks). We leave Goliath to someone else because he's too big for us, and that seems best. But attempting to insulate yourself is futile. For "who of you, by worrying, can add a single hour to your life? Since you cannot do this very little thing, why do you worry about the rest?"[13]

I'm aware there are natural fears that keep us safe:

Don't touch the oven.

Don't run out into the street.

Don't stand too close to the edge.

But the deep fears—the ones that really control us—rarely keep bad things from happening.

To quote another of David's Psalms: "...for You alone, O Lord, make me dwell in safety"[14]—not my plans or my common sense or my education.

You alone, O Lord! If God wants you to step out in faith, though it may lead you into the midst of a raging battle, you will find that His presence and His purpose grow stronger with each step.

So, if God's plan for real dangers is that we face them head-on and trust in His protection and purpose, what do you think He wants us to do with the imaginary ones we talked about at the beginning of the chapter?

---

13   Luke 12:25
14   Psalm 4:8

"Therefore, I tell you, do not be anxious about your life, what you will eat or what you will drink, nor about your body, what you will put on. Is not life more than food, and the body more than clothing? Look at the birds of the air: they neither sow nor reap nor gather into barns, and yet your heavenly Father feeds them. Are you not of more value than they? And which of you by being anxious can add a single hour to his span of life? And why are you anxious about clothing? Consider the lilies of the field, how they grow: they neither toil nor spin, yet I tell you, even Solomon in all his glory was not arrayed like one of these. But if God so clothes the grass of the field, which today is alive and tomorrow is thrown into the oven, will he not much more clothe you, O you of little faith? Therefore, do not be anxious, saying, 'What shall we eat?' or 'What shall we drink?' or 'What shall we wear?' For the Gentiles seek after all these things, and your heavenly Father knows that you need them all. But seek first the Kingdom of God and His righteousness, and all these things will be added to you."[15]

"Do not be anxious about anything, but in everything by prayer and supplication with thanksgiving let your requests be made known to God. And the peace of God, which surpasses all understanding, will guard your hearts and your minds in Christ Jesus."[16]

The natural response to fear of any kind—whether physical or emotional—is the fight-or-flight reaction which leaves you angry, anxious, and exhausted. If, instead, you train your mind to make fear a trigger for "prayer and supplication with thanksgiving," each new battle will become an opportunity to rely on God. Faith is a muscle, and this repetition of fear = prayer, fear = prayer, fear = prayer is exercise. It will breathe life into your relationship

[15] Matthew 6:25-33
[16] Philippians 4:6-7

with the Lord, helping you see Him more and more as the loving God He truly is. You will fight those inevitable battles as David did—with confidence in the Lord despite the strength of the giants that threaten.

If faith is a muscle, fear is what happens when that muscle atrophies from disuse. Until your weakness sends you to Him and Him alone, your fear will leave you more and more debilitated.

But turning to Him in your weakness converts it into strength.[17] Against all odds, you will defeat the lion, the bear, the Goliath, and bit by bit, you will build up that muscle.

Trusting God does not exempt us from trouble. John 16:33 says, "In the world, you will have tribulation. But take heart; I have overcome the world."

Your "Goliath" will come. You can cower from it, alone and uncertain, or you can choose to face it confidently with God at your side.

TAKEAWAYS:

- Fighting your lion or your bear or your Goliath will look crazy to others. It may even seem crazy to you at first, but the more you exercise your faith muscle in the small things, the more you will come to rely on God's guidance even when the risk seems reckless and foolhardy.
- Fear wants you to stay on the sidelines in the safe zone, but if you do, you never get the chance to exercise your faith muscle. And when Goliath comes, you will falter.
- Don't start with Goliath. Start with the coworker who makes you crazy, the anxiety-riddled mornings with

---

17 2 Corinthians 12:9-10

your kids, the sputter in your car's engine. Give God the chance to come through for you.
- If you are faithful along the way, God will trust you with more battles. At first, David was only protecting his father's sheep. When he met Goliath, he defended all of Israel—the Lord's sheep.
- You don't need to be the smartest or the strongest or to have the best army or the best plan to defeat your Goliath. You only need the Lord on your side and whatever He's entrusted you with. God loves to take down Goliaths with a pebble.
- Fear can trigger panic, or it can trigger prayer. Intentionally teaching yourself to turn to prayer when anxiety strikes will take away fear's power little by little.

SELF-SUFFICIENCY

Ten things undertaken for Christ at our own prompting will count for less than one thing done in His name at His bidding.

G.P. Pardington, *The Still Small Voice; Quiet Hour Talks*

Self-sufficiency is one of my biggest battles. I am a lone wolf, do-it-yourself, don't-ask-for-help kind of person. Where my spiritual life is concerned, it's really not the best trait. I push and push and push myself only to grow weary and exhausted and give up. Too often, instead of taking up my cross and following *Jesus*, I take up my cross and follow *myself*. I plan every minute, and give Him no room to move.

The truth is we often *want* to do it ourselves. Relying on someone else is scary, and it doesn't allow any room for pride. Let's face it, sometimes our ideas seem pretty darn good, and we don't bother checking with God before we make a royal mess—in Moses's case, a literal one.

Though raised as a son in Pharaoh's house, Moses knew where he came from, and the plight of his people weighed on him. He probably often thought of his unique place of authority and influence and the best way to use it to their advantage. I'm sure he considered all sorts of political moves and ways to curry personal favor—methods making good use of his worldly means and position. I know I would have.

When Moses came across the Egyptian guard beating the Hebrew slave, he decided he had to act, killing the guard and incurring Pharaoh's wrath in the process. Thus, began his wanderings. In the act of defending someone, Moses lost everything. He went too far, and his good intentions saw him cast out—all his earthly power and influence gone in a moment. Can you imagine his feelings of defeat and failure? He probably thought he had blown it. He was on the cusp of being able to do something great for the Israelites when one misguided action ruined his chance.

Thankfully, God's thoughts are not our thoughts, and His ways are not our ways.[18]

Forty years passed before God came back to Moses with a plan and led the Israelites out of slavery—forty years Moses probably spent thinking he'd missed his chance to do something big. But God didn't want Moses's position and power. He wanted his obedience.

You and I think we need the worldly means necessary to accomplish God's plans, and we often fall into despair if those means are stripped away, but when you feel confident in your money, your intelligence, your talent, or your position, it's easy to attribute success to yourself and your own abilities. It wouldn't have seemed very miraculous if Moses had diplomatically arranged the release of his people. But the way God did it in the end, with plagues and the parting of the Red Sea? No one could deny the hand of God in that situation.

18 Isaiah 55:8

It is never *your* abilities that need to be at the forefront, but God's. If you are perfectly equipped by worldly standards, no one can see God's hand moving.

I try to remind myself of this when I'm feeling inadequate. My experience tells me that most things God prompts me to do feel a bit like stepping off a cliff—writing, for instance. It's a giant leap into the great unknown.

When I sit down to write (a thing I know I am incapable of doing without the Lord's help), I suddenly find myself drawn to all the chores I've been putting off—things I don't even enjoy—simply because I feel capable of doing them. Wash the dishes, pay the bills, fold the laundry; I want things I can do on my own with very little risk of failure.

When, however, we step off the cliff into the tasks God has given us, we must totally rely on Him if they're to be done at all, and we don't like feeling reliant. We like to pretend we're in control.

It's ironic that we seem to think trusting God with our lives is more difficult and uncertain than shouldering the entire burden ourselves and hoping for the best. But we want a formula, and God isn't formulaic. What He has for us to do may seem irrelevant or pointless or humiliating. Noah endured over fifty years of ridicule for building a boat when it had never rained. God's tasks are often unconventional, and their outcomes rarely seem certain.

Being bold about my faith feels like that. Is it even making a difference?

Denying myself to follow Him feels like that. Is it worth it?

Writing feels like that. Do people think I'm crazy for trying?

But dishes are risk-free, I am confident in my bill-paying skills, and laundry feels like a thing I can do.

I can plod on in mediocrity and the mundane, never delve into God's plan for me, and blame the world and my circumstances for any lack of fulfillment I feel. That I can do quite well. But can I step off the cliff into the unknown God has planned for me and potentially wander in uncertainty and ridicule for forty years? Fifty years?

Like the Israelites, *being enslaved* feels like a thing I can do. They knew how to be slaves; they were perfectly capable of it all on their own. But they didn't know how to wander in the desert where they had to rely on God for absolutely everything.

When you enter God's realm, you find yourself walking blind, so to speak. And until you've been walking with Him for quite some time, it's difficult to trust that walking blind is worth it. It takes some exercising of that faith muscle I mentioned earlier.

Most of the Israelites lost hope despite the fact that God supplied their *every daily need*. He literally sent them bread from heaven and guided their path by fire and cloud, but they still didn't believe Him. This is eye-opening to me. Don't you often wish that God would just make things easy? He did that for the Israelites. They didn't have to worry a bit about their day-to-day needs, but they still weren't satisfied.

They lost hope in the destination—the Promised Land. Maybe they stopped thinking God knew what He was doing, or maybe they started thinking He didn't have their best interests at heart.

If I'm honest, I have to admit that I start to grumble in the desert, too. I can truly say I believe that "the sufferings of this present time are not worth comparing with the glory that is to be revealed to us,"[19] but I want to learn how to *live* like I believe it.

I want to walk in uncertainty through difficult times and times I feel useless and times I don't understand. I want to use

---

19   Romans 8:18

those circumstances to grow more intimate with the Lord. Even if there are years and years when I can't see the destination, I want to trust He's leading me right. It's easy to walk back into the mundane and the routine of my to-dos—in other words, to take up my cross and follow *myself* again.

But *it doesn't work.* I feel increasingly restless and empty and worthless despite checking the boxes and keeping up with life in a perfectly respectable manner.

God's plan often takes me off the beaten path to a place I'm uncomfortable and uncertain, and it very often *seems* to take me away from my desires. But even when I don't understand what He's doing, the days I follow His lead always end with me feeling full and at peace.

I'm actually not sure that stepping off the cliff—the initial flight from Egypt—is the hard part. I think a lot of people get that far. They don't *like* the slavery after all. But a few years into the wanderings, they give up and turn back.

I thought you'd do more than this, God. I didn't leave everything I knew for the wilderness and endless uncertainty.

Like the Israelites, we think we would've been better off if we'd stayed in Egypt. It feels like the Lord brought us out into the desert to starve.[20] But the reason they felt like they were starving is because they continued to seek things He did not want for them. They chose to be discontented with His provision.

In the desert—in *your* desert—God is your only chance for survival, for meaning, and for hope. The desert completely destroys even the illusion of being able to provide for yourself, but it is also full of HIM. Nowhere else can you more clearly see His work and His guidance. You can choose to dwell in the emptiness and your helplessness, or you can choose to dwell in the fullness of

[20] Exodus 16:3

His provision and His presence. You have to trust Him to rescue you and go on trusting Him through all the dry places and the valleys along the way.

Maybe you took a step of faith, but now you doubt the path.

The voice of the enemy whispers:

Nobody cares. You're not doing anyone any good. It's a waste of time. There's nothing here.

But if you listen, there is also God's voice:

Keep going. Trust Me. Follow Me through this desert. The Promised Land awaits. It's worth it.

Each time you die to yourself, God comes a little more alive in you. "He must increase, but I must decrease."[21]

Following God's guidance will rarely lead you where you would choose to go, because He can see beyond your limited vision. He can see if taking a detour here will change lives exponentially or be totally pointless. He can see if you should clean your house today or leave it in total disarray to hang out with a friend. He can see when you need to give of your time even if you're already feeling depleted or when you need to stay home, ignore all your checklists, and spend a day simply abiding in Him.

But you can't know any of that if you're not in communion with Him, and you won't do it if you don't trust Him. When you deny yourself and take up your cross and follow *yourself*—your own plans and agenda—everything feels like a burden. It will weigh you down and down and down until you have no more strength. But when you deny yourself and take up your cross and follow *Him*, He renews your strength, and you will "run and not be weary…walk and not faint."[22]

I have realized that I rarely know what will satisfy my soul and bring long-term good in my life, but *He always does*. And yet

---

21 John 3:30
22 Isaiah 40:31

I somehow keep attempting to live a life of faith under my own strength like a three-year-old yelling, "I do it myself!" when I've no business even trying. And just like that three-year-old, I don't understand that I must grow and learn and that it takes time and patience and perseverance.

I want to arrive before I have journeyed and to know before I have learned. But teleportation and osmosis work no better in the Christian walk than they do in the real world. The actual path requires a progression: "…suffering produces endurance, and endurance produces character, and character produces hope…."[23]

You may suffer in the desert, but that suffering will produce endurance, then character, and finally hope. Isn't it interesting that hope is an outflow of character? We don't think of "hope" as a moral objective. But we can only have hope in all circumstances if we're living lives of faith like Abraham who "…believed God, and it was counted to him as righteousness."[24]

The Bible commands us to hope in the Lord so many times. This is not a vain wish but is defined as an "expectation of what is certain." It's a sincere trust and a confident assurance.

The desert is where your hope in God will flourish because in it, He is all you can rely on. The longer you follow Him, the more of Him you will see—not because He changes, but because you do.

TAKEAWAYS:

- God's purpose doesn't require any worldly advantages you seem to have. If you lose those advantages, He can still bring his plan for you to fruition.

23 Romans 5:3-4
24 Genesis 15:6

- Your own abilities are, in fact, often a distraction keeping you from trusting God and keeping others from seeing God's hand at work.
- God often has a plan you would never pick and can't understand, because it's impossible with our human limitations.
- God's path often looks meandering, aimless, or terrifying, but if you trust Him while you're on it, you will be both closer to Him and more fulfilled along the way.
- You often have to grow into His calling for you, and that growth may require suffering, but out of suffering, He produces hope.

DOUBT

When it comes to our own walk with God, we can have faith and still have doubt. Faith is getting out of the boat and walking on the water even though you have doubts.

Michael R. Licona

Before we get into the meat of this chapter, I want to briefly address doubt as it pertains to intellectual concerns. Those doubts are not something to be ashamed of or ignored, but a reason to delve deeper into the underlying truths of Christianity. There are many *surface* inconsistencies in cultural Christianity that lead people away from Christ, but I've found that those who don't stop there, but study, dig deep, and really want truth come out with a faith richer than they began with. I don't cover this type of doubt in my discussion here, but I didn't want to ignore it completely.[25][26][27][28][29]

---

25 Deuteronomy 4:29
26 Proverbs 8:17
27 Jeremiah 29:13
28 Matthew 7:7
29 Luke 11:9

You might be thinking that doubt is a lot like fear, and you'd be right, but the difference is substantial enough to explore.

We *fear* bad things, but we *doubt* good things.

The doubt appears when you're just about to follow God into the murky unknown—a journey you know you can't make without Him. You're on the verge of leaving your Egypt, but the enemy is dogging your steps, and the only thing you can see ahead of you is the desert. You've planned for the trip, gathered your gear, and started to walk when doubt sneaks in the back door and tries to ruin your hope.

God's not really going to show up.
Who do you think you are?
Do you really think you heard Him?
You should just go back.

God frequently asks you to take a first step before you even see Him begin to move. You have to take a risk, put yourself out there, show your proverbial hand. If God doesn't come through, the whole world will know. You'll be a fool, a failure, a pariah, or even, possibly, dead.

I'm reminded of that scene near the end of *Indiana Jones and the Last Crusade* when Indy needs to cross the chasm. He remembers the clue: "The Path of God—only in the leap from the lion's head will he prove his worth." He knows the path *should* be there, but his eyes say it's not. He takes the step anyway—his need is great, and time is of the essence—and it turns out the path was there all along. He just couldn't see it from his perspective.

It's that "hope in what you do not see"[30] Paul talks about. God wants you to believe. Not just to *say* you believe when the path is clear, but to continue believing—and acting like it—even when you're in the dark. Anyone can believe if they've seen God

---

30 Romans 8:25

blaze the trail before them miraculously, and sometimes, He does just that, as when He parted the Red Sea for the Israelites.[31] But God knows if your faith is only in signs and wonders and flashy demonstrations, you will eventually stray. You will fall for the next neat trick, and any impressive display will turn you away from Him.

So, He asks you to trust when the signs are still unclear and all you have is the whisper of His still, small voice.[32] There are many biblical examples of this.

In John 4, the nobleman asked for his son to be healed just after Jesus said, "Unless you people see signs and wonders, you will by no means believe." Jesus answered the nobleman, "Go your way; your son lives," and gave him no sign or proof. The man obeyed. Don't you imagine he was tempted to say, "But how do I know, Lord?" Don't you think he feared arriving home and finding his son no better, or perhaps, even dead? But still, he journeyed home in faith, hoping on the promise he was given.

In Joshua 3, God instructed the people to follow the priests to the banks of the Jordan where the waters would not part until the soles of their feet were *already in the water.* That means six-hundred thousand people stood, packed and ready to pass through a place where there *was no way.*

Don't you wonder what they thought—what they felt? Were they passing furtive glances back and forth, uncertain God would come through? But He "made a way in the wilderness."[33]

And what about in Luke 5:4 when Jesus said to Simon Peter, "Launch out into the deep, and let your nets down for a catch?" Jesus called him to *the deep.* Not to the shallows. There is danger

---

31   Exodus 14:21
32   I Kings 19:12
33   Isaiah 43:19

in the deep, and getting there requires time and effort—time and effort Peter had already expended.

"But we have toiled all night and caught nothing, Lord," Peter said. I can imagine him shrugging here before he continued, "But at your word...."[34]

I love this picture. How many times have I cast my net and come up empty? I've sat down to write and found no words. The well is dry. I should give up. I can't do this.

"But at your word...."

Don't launch out because you're bucking up your courage and think you'll give it another go or because general wisdom tells you not to give up or because you're not willing to fail. I do that more often than I'd like to admit, and it only leads to disappointment and exhaustion. Peter didn't just step out of the boat to join Jesus walking on the water. *He asked Jesus to tell him to, then waited for an invitation.*[35] He knew it may not be God's will for him to step out of the boat. *But at His word,* Peter took the step of faith.

If the Israelites had tried to free themselves from Egypt and struck out into the desert before God told them to, they'd have been crushed, drowned, starved, and alone.

But when we follow, *at His word,* Jesus shows up. "Launch out into the deep," He says.

But I just came from there, God, we think. *It was useless. I tried all day/night/week/year.*

There are no fish.

There are no words.

My daughter's still mad at me.

I have no strength, no hope, nothing to give.

But in an act of faith, we catch our doubt and say, "Nevertheless, at Your word..."

---

34   Luke 5:5
35   Matthew 14: 25-29

I will let down my net.
I will pick up my pen.
I will speak life to my children.
I will take the next step.

And though you doubt, God comes through. Your nets are full—more fish than you've ever seen. The page fills up—words with depth and heart I know couldn't have come from my depleted soul. Your children relax into your arms despite all the words spoken in anger. The next step reveals the bridge you could not see from where you stood.

Doubt is only a problem when you let it turn you away from Jesus. When Peter joined Jesus to walk on the water, he was fine until he turned to face his circumstances instead of looking at Christ.

But even then, when you step out in faith but still wrestle with doubt, there comes a tender reassurance.

Jesus stretched out His hand to lift Peter up when he began to sink.

Jesus reached out His scarred hand to assuage Thomas's uncertainty—"See my hands. Reach out your hand and put it into my side. Stop doubting and believe…."

Jesus freed the tormented child in Mark 9 when the father said, "I believe; help my unbelief."

Jesus did not reprimand here; He encouraged.

There *are* times when doubt results in rebuke. Sarah was scolded for laughing at the idea of having a child, while Abraham was reassured when he expressed doubt. Zechariah was reprimanded and struck temporarily unable to speak for questioning how he and Elizabeth would conceive, while Mary was given an explanation when she asked the same thing.

Maybe these were differentiated because Sarah and Zechariah doubted whether God *could* do a thing rather than whether He *would,* and put limits on what they felt God was capable of. Whatever the reasons, I'm sure the heart and motives behind their doubts were a factor.

What I do know is this—God rejoices when we believe. In Romans 4, Abraham is counted as righteous because he *believed God.*

I think we often see this belief as a passive acceptance of Christ's identity, but we need to take it in context with the way Abraham believed God—leaving his home and all he knew, not knowing where he was going.[36] This belief is about living your life in such a way that believing Him is evident. We trust His promises, and we take those leaps of faith when He gives the word.

When Peter focused on the threatening circumstances around him, he began to sink, but when he looked back to Jesus, he was raised up out of the waves. The Israelites chose not to look back at God when they began to flounder, but continued wallowing in constant fear of their worldly situation. They wanted earthly solutions, and they were not allowed to enter God's rest because their unbelief led to disobedience, hardened hearts, rebellion, and ultimately, a total departure from God.[37]

Hebrews 11—the "Faith Chapter"—is a rollcall of the faithful elite—all praised for believing in what they could not see. I take heart in the fact that many of the people listed in this chapter had biblically documented episodes of doubt.

Your doubt may cause you to sink in your circumstances for a time, but unlike the Israelites, *it doesn't have to keep you there.*

Temporary doubt is inevitable; we are human, but Jesus's hand is always outstretched. All you need to do is look to Him

---

36 Hebrews 11:8
37 Hebrews 3:19

and take it. He will raise you up when you turn back to Him. He wants you to believe, but His grace covers your doubt. Never hesitate to turn to Him, and "hold fast the confidence and the rejoicing of the hope firm to the end."[38]

TAKEAWAYS:
- Doubt is Satan's effort to derail you when you're on the verge of taking that leap of faith. He wants to destroy your hope!
- God often asks us to take the first step without any outward assurance except His call. That step is often uncertain, difficult, and, sometimes, even dangerous.
- Don't wait for signs and wonders if you know you've heard His voice or felt His leading.
- But don't head out into the wilderness or try walking on water if He hasn't called you there! You'll only end up broken and exhausted.
- God may call you to something you've already been doing unsuccessfully. Peter—an experienced fisherman—had been fishing all night and caught nothing until Jesus told him to "launch out into the deep." Don't resist a call because you "already tried that" and it didn't work.
- Doubting does not keep you from walking in His will unless you remain in it. If you reach for Him, He will take your hand and lead you back every time.

38 Hebrews 3:6

PLEASURE

It would seem that our Lord finds our desires not too strong, but too weak. We are half-hearted creatures, fooling about with drink and sex and ambition when infinite joy is offered us, like an ignorant child who wants to go on making mud pies in a slum because he cannot imagine what is meant by the offer of a holiday at the sea. We are far too easily pleased.[39]

C.S. Lewis, *The Weight of Glory*

Earlier today, one of my cats was begging for a treat. My husband (a big softie) caved after telling her, "OK, but if you get a treat now, you won't get your midnight snack."

"She only knows what she wants right now," I said. "She doesn't understand 'later,'" (As if she understood the rest of it.) "Humans barely understand 'later.'"

And that little story encapsulates why we let short-term pleasure get in the way of the true inheritance God has for us.

39   *The Weight of Glory* by C.S. Lewis © Copyright C.S. Lewis Pte Ltd 1949. Extract reprinted by permission.

Our flesh is weak.[40] It wants what it wants, and it wants it now. When the reward seems too far off, we hardly believe it's real. Like the Israelites in the desert, it's easy to focus on the immediacy of our want and forget all about the Promised Land. God's promise feels ephemeral and distant, like the telescopic photograph of a galaxy. It's beautiful, but difficult to connect to our lives in any meaningful way.

And too often, we turn away from Him and attempt to fill our lives with earthly things—things we can taste and touch and see.

The prodigal son[41] had an inheritance meant to provide for him forever. It wasn't just money; it was a loving father making provision for his son's future.

We all know that the son took his portion and squandered it in decadence and debauchery, but remember, this inheritance would have included livestock and property and buildings. To live this way and end up with nothing, the son had to *sell everything his father had given him,* trading away the future his father had worked so hard to give for a pleasure that did not last.

Every bit of inheritance we try to wrest from this world instead of trusting in the inheritance God provides is the equivalent of selling pieces of the eternal bounty and purpose God wants for us, wasting His gift and intent for our lives in pursuit of fleeting pleasures that can never satisfy.

I may not be squandering my money on lewd living and depravity, but how often am I the prodigal son in my own living room, trading eternal things for the temporal? I would wager never a full day passes that I don't choose some earthly pleasure over God's purpose for my life, selling bits from my imperishable, unfading inheritance to purchase a little pleasure today. For me, it

---

40   Matthew 26:41
41   Luke 15:11-32

often looks like too many snacks when I'm stressed or a plethora of excuses to avoid doing things that stretch me.

What about you?

Maybe you are restless and tired, so you binge-watch your favorite show instead of contacting the friend God laid on your heart.

Maybe you are irritable after a bad day at work, so you eat a whole package of Oreos instead of taking it to God in prayer or dealing with the issue.

Maybe you are lonely and feeling insecure, so you turn to an unhealthy relationship for validation.

Maybe you find your identity in your work or your finances or man's approval or even some noble purpose, and you're only happy when it's going well.

Maybe you seek solace in a bottle, do a little retail therapy, scroll social media, or disappear into a book.

Maybe, maybe, maybe…

If you chase those maybes to find your happiness and peace, this is what I know:

1) They won't work.

2) They'll leave you worse off than you started.

Tempting us to seek our reward on this earth is a cruel trick the devil likes to play. He promises delight but delivers emptiness, for "whoever seeks to save his life will lose it, and whoever loses his life will preserve it."[42]

Like the prodigal son, we forget the wonder of who our Father is, His perfect love, and the eternal reward He offers. Pursuing worldly pleasure is an act of turning away from Him that keeps us from experiencing the true depth and intimacy He wants

---

42 Luke 17:33

with us—the very intimacy that will produce the fulfillment we so desperately seek.

We don't consider that we're trading overflowing fountains of eternal living water for broken cisterns and empty wells.[43]

If the prodigal son didn't convince you of this, maybe Solomon will. Commonly considered the wisest man who ever lived, he did what I call a "fulfillment experiment." (Though I'd like to think the wisest man who ever lived wouldn't *have* to conduct such an experiment.)

Uniquely placed with wealth and position, Solomon had the ability to test it all. "Whatever my eyes desired I did not keep from them. I did not withhold my heart from any pleasure, for my heart rejoiced in all my labor; and this was my reward from all my labor. Then I looked on all the works that my hands had done and on the labor in which I had toiled; and indeed, all was vanity and grasping for the wind. There was no profit under the sun."[44]

Solomon tried seeking purpose in work and wealth and power and learning and self-indulgence and still concluded that *all is vanity and grasping for the wind.*

There's a part of you (and me!) that thinks, *Yeah, but I mean… is it really? Everything I want? Anything I want? I'm pretty sure I could be happy…*

…if I had enough money.
…if I got that job.
…if I had that master's degree.
…if I could take that vacation.

We can insert any "if" we want, but unless it's part of what God has for us and we pursue it through His guidance, it will be no more fulfilling than grasping for the wind.

43 Jeremiah 2:13
44 Ecclesiastes 2:10-11

In the past year, this truth has become real to me. For the first time in my life, we are financially secure. I'm self-employed and have work that is meaningful and rewarding. To a large extent, I'm now able to carve out time for writing and art the way I've always wanted. I'm happily married and healthy. I'm checking all the boxes here—finances, meaningful work, relationships, health.

But despite achieving goals I've strived for my entire life, emotionally, it's been one of my toughest years.

Part of that difficulty arose when I realized I'd still been living under the guise of "I'll be happy when…." Though intellectually and biblically I know this to be false, part of me still believed things would magically become easy and wonderful and perfect once my circumstances aligned with my desires.

And now that I'm here, I finally *feel* it—this grasping for the wind. None of this filled the hole, and it never will. Money and relationships and work will never be enough.

Isn't it sad how many lessons we have to learn the hard way? I could've been sitting at the feet of the Father all along—trusting His plan, looking to Him for fulfillment, and resting in Him instead of grasping and striving to reach a goal I thought would satisfy me.

The good news is that no matter how long or how often we chase the wrong things or how far away we go, the Father always welcomes us back with open arms and celebration.

The only thing we need—the only thing that *can* fulfill us—is God and our faith and obedience to Him. "Find rest, O my soul, in God alone; my hope comes from Him. He alone is my rock and my salvation…."[45]

[45] Psalm 62:5-6

Jesus Christ is the Living Water who will always satisfy. Feeding our fleshly desires will only ever curb our emptiness momentarily, never quench it. So when we're feeling disgruntled, defeated, and discouraged, how do we refresh our commitment to God and His eternal reward?

By following Asaph's example in Psalm 73. His faith had faltered. He was envious of the wicked. They seemed to get everything they wanted. Why did he bother being righteous? It didn't make his life any easier.

Asaph's natural inclination was to give up and turn to other things for a reward, but look what he did in verses 16-17: "…it seemed to me a wearisome task, until I went into the sanctuary of God…."

He took the matter to the Lord.

He was reminded that those who are far from God will perish in the end. He remembered that God was his refuge, his strength, and his portion—his *inheritance*. And that the inheritance is *worth the wait.* "…There is nothing on earth that I desire besides You," he said in Psalm 73:25. His faith was renewed in fellowship with the Father.

The deeper we grow in our relationship with God, the more our fleshly desires will fade, because we will see His worth and experience His satisfaction. Our minds and hearts will grow used to mining for the lasting things of God. Diamonds are never on the surface. The worldly things that seem like easy joy or quick fixes are always fakes.

This world is not our home: "For here we have no lasting city, but we seek the city that is to come."[46] When you are tired

---
46   Hebrews 13:14

and tempted in the flesh, "do not grow weary of doing good, for in due season you will reap, if you do not give up."[47]

Rather than trading our inheritance for fleeting pleasures like the prodigal son did, I pray we become like the man who found the treasure—the Kingdom of Heaven—in a field. He sold all his earthly goods to purchase it, because he understood its infinite, all-encompassing worth. I'm reminded of the quote by missionary Jim Elliot: "He is no fool who gives what he cannot keep to gain that which he cannot lose." The Kingdom of God is worth *everything—HE* is worth everything. All earthly treasures pale in comparison.

Even Oreos.

TAKEAWAYS:
- Your flesh will always choose the short-term reward, because that is its nature.
- Every time you seek satisfaction in an earthly reward, you rob your soul of a bit of the true eternal satisfaction God has for you.
- Walking towards fleshly rewards in search of fulfillment is walking away from God—the very thing that provides that fulfillment.
- All earthly pursuits—even positive ones—are as grasping at the wind unless they are done through God's guidance.
- God's inheritance is worth the wait; His living water satisfies all the needs you try to fulfill in the flesh.
- This world is not our home; seeking our reward here doesn't make sense if we truly believe God's promise for the Kingdom of Heaven.

---

47   Galatians 6:9

- No matter how many times you choose the flesh over Him, God is always overjoyed to welcome you back.
- When you feel the urge to satisfy your emptiness in the flesh, that's the time to seek fellowship with God. He will remind you of truth and fill you with His presence, His love, and His goodness.

ABANDONMENT

Wherever the providence of God may dump us down, in a slum, in a shop, in the desert, we have to labour along the line of His direction. Never allow this thought—'I am of no use where I am,' because you certainly can be of no use where you are not!

Oswald Chambers, *So Send I You*[48]

Alone. Unsheltered. Betrayed.

That's what I think of when I say the word *abandoned*. It's a personal, painful place to live.

I would've said it's not something I struggle with. I wasn't abandoned, after all. But when I started writing this chapter, I was in a room full of other authors during a writing blitz at a retreat, and God began a work of healing I didn't know I needed. Among the clitter-clatter of keys and the scratch of pens, my silent tears began to fall. I felt like God took me into his arms and spoke the words:

---

[48] Taken from *So Send I You* by Oswald Chambers, © 1930 by Oswald Chambers Publications Assn., Ltd., and used by permission of Our Daily Bread Publishing, Grand Rapids, MI 49501. All rights reserved.

I'm with you.[49] *I'll fight for you.*[50] *I'll protect you.*[51] *I'll take care of you.*[52]

I grew up in a Christian home where I always knew I was loved, but every family has its issues. Our lives were never quite stable or normal, and I felt a lot of uncertainty. Between financial troubles and a parent with mental health issues, it never felt like I had anything to depend on. I know many people had more difficult childhoods, and trust me, I'm grateful for the love, the faith, and the work ethic we were trained up into. I'm also very thankful there was no physical abuse, but my upbringing still fueled me with a determination to never be at anyone else's mercy. I wasn't inclined to trust others with any amount of control over my life.

That distrust extended even to God and kept me entrenched in fighting my own battles, making my own path, and never *quite* believing that God would come through.

There are so many Bible stories that encourage me to trust even when I feel God isn't near, but foremost is the story of Joseph. Talk about being alone, abandoned, and betrayed by those who should've protected him!

Joseph was only seventeen when he was sold into slavery by his *older brothers*. Can you imagine the trauma? His siblings were so jealous, they *sold him*. The Bible doesn't delve into Joseph's emotions in this story, *but how would you have felt?*

I can answer for myself.

Angry. Confused. Hopeless. Despairing. Destitute. Worthless. Unwanted. Lost. And everything I said above: alone, unsheltered, and betrayed.

---

49 Hebrews 13:5
50 Exodus 14:14
51 Psalm 121:7
52 Philippians 4:19

This came on the heels of Joseph's dreams of greatness. I doubt he followed his captors into the dusty horizon with a song of thankfulness in his heart. I bet he wrestled with God—and not just a little.

But sometime along the way, Joseph decided to be the person God wanted him to be despite his circumstances. He decided to live a life of integrity, prayer, and trust.

So, he worked his way up to become the manager of a notable household. His master trusted him with everything. God was blessing his diligence.

And then came the crash—another betrayal just as things seemed to be coming together.

Potiphar's wife tried to seduce him, and upon failing, accused him of rape. This was a woman he'd never wronged.

When his brothers sold him, maybe Joseph even held himself somewhat accountable for their anger (though the punishment certainly didn't fit the crime). He *had* been talking about that dream,[53] after all; maybe he'd been a little full of himself.

But this? He was doing the right thing the right way. He was above reproach, but the downfall came anyway.

I love Joseph's words when he refused Potiphar's wife: "How then could I do such a wicked thing and sin against God?"[54]

We would say the sin would be against Potiphar, but Joseph understood what was really at stake. This would not only be shameful to his earthly position but to his heavenly one.

It's easy for me to forget the eternal consequences of sin rather than just consider the earthly ones, but Joseph went straight to it, and because he wanted to be right before God's eyes instead of just man's, he was disgraced and betrayed. *Again.*

---

53 Genesis 37:5-11
54 Genesis 39:9

It would have been so easy for Joseph to become bitter—to be mad at God. Maybe he was, but if so, we know it didn't last, because the cycle repeated.

Joseph was honorable and reliable. He worked his way up in the prison. He was trusted by the guards. He interpreted the dreams of a fellow prisoner who should have remembered to mention him to Pharaoh, but didn't.

Where would you be in your faith journey at this point? Maybe once again angry, confused, and hopeless.

I shudder to think. I find it difficult to let go and trust God when someone insults me unfairly or accuses me of something I didn't do even when it has no consequences whatsoever. If my family sold me into slavery, someone unfairly imprisoned me for a crime I didn't commit, then a person I helped left me to rot in prison for years, I can't imagine how shattered I'd be.

I would bet money Joseph struggled through these feelings, yet somehow, he remained faithful.

I wonder how often he pondered that first dream—the one where his family bowed to him—and wondered what God was doing. He was still interpreting the dreams of others, so he hadn't lost the belief that God spoke in that way.

Thirteen years of slavery and prison and abandonment.

Did God give you a dream? Maybe years have passed, and you wonder if you imagined it, got confused, misunderstood. The years have been full of pain and betrayal, and no matter what you do, you hit setback after setback. You've been battered by the world, by the enemy.

But maybe God's not done, just like He wasn't done with Joseph. When Pharaoh needed a dream interpreter, the cupbearer suddenly remembered: *Hey, there was this guy in prison....*

Joseph's time had come. And because he'd been listening to God, following "in the desert," all along, he was prepared. This was his Goliath. What if he hadn't been ready? What if he'd been mad at God and languishing in captivity instead of "working as for the Lord?"[55] Would he still have been able to interpret Pharaoh's dream? Maybe.

I know God's success is not dependent on our faithfulness or even our obedience. Perhaps, like Jonah who ran from God, the Lord would have brought him into obedience. Perhaps, like Abraham and Sarah, Joseph would have come back around to his faith after a time of doubt and still been counted as righteous. We can't know.

What I *do* know is that following that path would have left Joseph floundering along the way. If he'd been angry at God and trying to shut Him out because of his suffering, he would've missed the joy of the Lord's guidance.

I often look back at seasons I didn't like and suddenly see what God was doing. What if I stopped waiting until trials were in my hindsight to trust Him? What if I trusted Him *now* and "counted it all joy when I met trials of all kinds, knowing that the testing of my faith produces perseverance, and at the end of perseverance comes *perfection*—a lack of nothing?"[56] We know this "lacking nothing" doesn't mean we will be sinless, nor does it mean we will have everything we want or never be in need. I think it goes back to that "all" we will have when we seek Him first.[57] The "all" is HIM—the intimacy, the rest, the fullness of a relationship with Him gives us the "peace that passes all understanding."[58] Joseph sure seemed to have that, though I'm sure he had his moments.

55 Colossians 3:23
56 James 1:2-4
57 Matthew 6:33
58 Philippians 4:7

But finally, God's plan had come clear. The famine was coming, and Pharaoh put Joseph in charge.

I love the restoration in this story. Joseph was given authority and power and, once again, proved himself an invaluable asset to the people he served. He rose to become *second* in charge of all of Egypt. That's a great restoration, but it's not all I'm talking about.

I'm talking about his family. The betrayers. His first heartbreak. It had been twenty-two years since he'd seen his family.

When I put myself in his shoes, I am crushed by the emotions that must have struck him as his brothers appeared. The story of how he contrived to get them to bring the rest of the family back to Egypt is long, but in it, we see his brokenness, his loneliness, his hope, and possibly, even a little of his anger.[59]

The healing of his deepest wound began that day. God had restored his freedom, his integrity, and now, his family.

The truth is we don't always get a neatly wrapped (albeit long-time-coming) restoration like this in our own lives. There is restoration—of that you can be sure—but it may not come so prettily.

Sometimes the restoration is internal. Perhaps someone betrayed and abandoned you. They may never apologize or deserve your forgiveness. The forgiveness is part of *your* restoration, not theirs. You don't need them to be a part of it. Sometimes, God will work the miracle the way He did for Joseph, but it's not required for your healing.

Letting go of earthly abandonment may be a thing you grapple with all your life. That doesn't mean it has to control you any more than it controlled Joseph. You can start from where you are and move forward.

I have a friend who struggled to forgive a past hurt. She prayed and prayed, but found the anger returning time after time.

---

59   Genesis 42:6-45:28

But anger is just a feeling. Having it is not a sin. It's what you do with it. It's a temptation in your mind and your heart, but it doesn't have to entice you to action. "But each person is tempted when he is lured and enticed by his own desire. Then desire when it has conceived gives birth to sin, and sin when it is fully grown brings forth death."[60] Your desire for justice and revenge tempts you, but it only becomes sin when you allow it to fester, germinate, and grow.

The feeling of anger and hurt may come every day, but if you choose to give it to the Lord over and over, you are still forgiving that hurt, and healing from it will come bit by bit.

I forgive. I forgive. I forgive.

I wonder how often Joseph had to repeat that in his prayers.

We can see by how he lived his life that he did not let bitterness or anger take root and be born. He was humble, accepted the painful path God placed him on, and came out the other side the second most powerful man in the world with a more beautiful story than he could ever have imagined.

So, if your hurt is looming large and your emptiness and abandonment is filling you with anger and bitterness, turn it over to God. Allow Him to redeem your heart and your soul in the midst of your pain. Don't wait till you are on the other side of it. Take the first step to becoming the person of faith and righteousness and integrity He's called you to be despite the obstacles and your seeming powerlessness. You can be who God wants you to be no matter where you are placed. Redeeming your hurts is His specialty!

---

60   James 1:14-15

TAKEAWAYS:
- Earthly abandonments and betrayals are often the beginning of God's greatest work in your life, *not* His failure to protect you as it might seem.
- Walking in righteousness may seem to have no pay-off at all in the moment. In fact, it may have terrible consequences. But the *ultimate* reward will always be ahead of us—on earth, an incomparable intimacy with God, and eventually Heaven, which will be a gift so glorious, we will wonder why we ever considered anything else worthy to compare.
- People may forget you, but God never does. He knows where you're going and how to get you there even when you are powerless and without hope—probably *especially* then.
- Your feelings about being abandoned and betrayed do not have to define or control you, no matter how long they persist. Hand them to God every time they arise, and allow Him to fill the void. Replace your inner voice with His.
- God is sovereign, and there is no situation too big for Him to transform to good and to His glory.
- One day, we will all be able to look back and see His purpose and plan. Don't wait for hindsight! Trust Him today, in the midst of the story. You don't know its end, but He does.

INSUFFICIENCY

God is looking for those with whom He can do the impossible. What a pity that we plan only the things that we can do by ourselves.

A.W. Tozer

At a writer's retreat I attended recently, someone said, "I don't understand why God called me to do something I can't do!" She couldn't imagine why God hadn't given the task to someone else—someone with more skill, more intelligence, more time, more patience…just *more*.

I feel that way sometimes. Each new chapter I write exposes another weakness in me. I war against self-doubt every time I sit down to type. It wants me to give up. It wants me to go do something easy that I feel confident in and leave this job to the big kids.

What about you? Maybe God called you to go back to school, adopt a child, lead a Bible study, write a book of your own, or witness to a co-worker. Maybe your first thought was, *I can't do that!*

I'm not smart enough.
I don't have enough room.
I don't have enough time.
I don't have enough money.

I'm not spiritual enough.
I'm just not enough.

The beauty of this is that even if those things are true—and they often are—GOD is enough, and He will make anything enough as long as are willing to trust Him with it all.

Have you ever really thought about the little boy with the five loaves and two fish?[61] Jesus told the disciples to feed the crowd—an impossible task. They didn't have any food or enough money to buy it.

I'm fictionalizing a bit, but I presume they went around asking people in the crowd, "Hey, do you have any food you could share?"

Only one little boy volunteered his lunch, and it *clearly* wasn't enough—not even a drop in the bucket compared to the number of people.

In a crowd upwards of five thousand, I'd be surprised if that boy was the only one with food—maybe some traveler provisioned for the beginning of a journey or some mama with snacks for her little ones. I can imagine them thinking:

This won't make a difference. It's not enough.

So, they stayed quiet—maybe not out of selfishness, but because they didn't understand what God could do with their inconsequential offerings—their "not-enoughs."

But God doesn't need you to be enough, have enough, or give enough. He only needs you to offer up what you have just like that little boy did.

I love his childlike faith. He didn't stop to consider that it might be silly to offer so little. He didn't second guess or hesitate, wondering what people would think or whether what he

---

61 John 6:9

had would make a difference. He just knew they were looking for food, and he had some.

And look at the results! His "not-enough" fed a crowd, and he became part of a miracle.

So many of us freeze when God calls. We think we can't possibly make a difference with our "not-enough-ness," so we don't offer anything. We stay quiet. Someone else has more, can offer more, can do more.

It's easy to use your inadequacy as an excuse, but that's when insecurity has become disobedience, feeding the self-doubt that's paralyzing you.

This is a spiral the devil absolutely loves. It keeps us inactive, ashamed, disobedient, and focused on ourselves instead of Jesus. We never see God's power because we are living in the shadow of our lack. We let it define us and determine what we are willing to do for the Lord, and we deprive ourselves the honor and beauty of being part of His miracle.

When God asks something seemingly impossible, and you think, "I can't do that," you're really saying, "*He* can't do that."

He can't turn my five loaves and two fishes into dinner for a multitude.

He can't provide financially for that child He wants me to adopt.

He can't give me the words to write that book.

But He *can!*

Our lack should always point us to God and end in faith rather than point us to ourselves and end in fear.

"Has He said, and will He not do it? Or has He spoken, and will He not fulfill it?"[62]

God is the God of being enough!

---

[62] Numbers 23:19b

God will very likely call you to do many things you are incapable of, because it's not your capabilities that matter. And you're in good company:

Could Moses have parted the sea?[63]

Could Daniel have closed the lions' mouths?[64]

Could the little boy have fed a multitude?

No! Their *obedience*—not their wisdom or strength or wealth—was transformed into a miracle.

You don't have to be wise or powerful or important in order to be chosen.

"Not many of you were wise by human standards; not many were influential; not many were of noble birth. But God chose the foolish things of the world to shame the wise; God chose the weak things of the world to shame the strong."[65]

That grand vision He gave you—the thing you want to see come about—is what He can do through your *obedience*. It's not that you suddenly find you really DID have enough time, money, endurance, spiritual maturity, or intelligence all along. It's that God transforms what you have into something amazing.

He transforms water into wine, ashes into beauty, foolishness into wisdom, weakness into strength.

And He transforms *you*.

He transforms everything that makes you incapable, unworthy, or inadequate into something He can use to great purpose. Nothing He's asked of you will be wasted in the Kingdom of Heaven even if, on its own, it seems woefully inadequate. When you believe His promise and act on it, He takes that faith and allows you to be a part of what *HE* is doing. Every tiny crumb you offer up to God is multiplied into bounty at His table.

---

63 Exodus 14:21
64 Daniel 6:22
65 I Corinthians 1:26-29

What miracle could you be a part of if you stopped telling God—and yourself—that what you have to offer isn't enough?

Instead of letting your weaknesses control you, rather, become like Paul and boast in them that the power of Christ may rest upon you, for "His strength is made perfect in weakness."

So, next time you hear the voice of God asking if anyone has food to feed His people, offer whatever scraps you have in your soul's cupboard, no matter how bare. Don't let your insufficiency hold you back.

For I am certain "that He who began a good work in you will bring it to completion at the day of Jesus Christ."[66]

God begins the work, and God completes it. It's all Him from the beginning to the end.

What freedom there is in knowing that your "not-enoughness" does not determine the fulfillment of God's plans! He takes whatever you have and multiplies it beyond "all you could ask or think."[67]

God is the God of being *more* than enough!

TAKEAWAYS:

- God will call you to things you feel incapable of doing—things you *are* incapable of doing. Don't worry about that; He knows everything about your abilities and your circumstances.
- God will transform your obedience into miracles.
- Don't use your insufficiency as an excuse. Be a part of His work by giving what you have.

66 Philippians 1:6
67 Ephesians 3:20

- When you can't, God CAN. Our lack should not keep us in inactivity and fear, but should lead us to faith that God is able regardless of our capabilities and resources.
- You don't have to be enough. His strength is made perfect in your weakness.
- The devil wants you to focus on your inadequacy instead of God's ability. He wants to keep you immobilized in insecurity. Don't let him win!
- God begins the work in you, and God completes it! Rest in His promise!

FAILURE

It's Satan's delight to tell me that once he's got me, he will keep me. But at that moment I can go back to God. And I know that if I confess my sins, God is faithful and just to forgive me.

Alan Redpath

"I can't do it perfectly, so I'm not going to do it at all."

A friend of mine once said those words about Christianity.

Like Paul, he "did not do the good he wanted, but the evil he did not want is what he kept on doing."[68]

Whereas Paul's failure reinforced his total dependence on Christ, my friend could only focus on himself and his own weakness. He couldn't handle feeling flawed and defeated, so he gave up.

We might not go that far, but when we fail our commitment to Christ, isn't our first reaction to run from Him? Like Adam and Eve in the Garden of Eden, we don't want to face His rebuke or our shame, so we hide.[69]

68 Romans 7:19
69 Genesis 3:8

And the hiding brings separation, and the separation keeps us from feeling His presence, and when we can't feel His presence, we drift further and further away.

This is the opposite of what God wants us to do when we fail, even when we fail big—probably *especially* when we fail big, like Peter.

Just before they went to the Garden of Gethsemane, Jesus warned him: "Peter, the rooster will not crow this day until you deny three times that you know Me."[70]

Peter protested, "Even if I must die with You, I will not deny You!"

He was so sure he would stay faithful—so confident in his own strength. But when Jesus was arrested and dying with Him became a real possibility, Peter's strength failed. "I do not know Him," he said. Three times he swore he didn't know this man he'd followed and loved for three years.

Don't you wonder if Peter had forgotten the conversation he had with Jesus earlier? Or was he so caught up in the moment that it didn't cross his mind? Either way, when the rooster crowed, Jesus turned and looked Peter in the eye, and he remembered.

That look must've been crushing—recalling Jesus's warning and his own arrogant response. He'd wanted to follow Jesus to the end, and what had he done instead? Lied. Saved his own skin. Turned away from the man he loved and knew to be the Messiah.

In grief and shame, Peter ran out into the courtyard where Jesus could no longer see him and wept.

I'm so glad the story doesn't end there. Instead, we get one of the most poignant, beautiful stories of restoration in the Bible. But first, we see Peter give up.

[70] Matthew 26:34-35

After Christ's death, a few of the disciples were standing around talking about what they were going to do next.

"I'm going fishing," Peter said, and a couple of the others joined him.

Fishing doesn't sound so bad until we remember that Jesus had called him *away* from it to become a "fisher of men." But Peter thought he'd failed Christ and failed his calling, so he went back to his old ways, his old life.

Maybe you think you've failed God's calling. He invited you to something new and exciting, but you've let Him down. Maybe it's a recurring sin you know He wants rooted from your life. Maybe it's that huge, one-time screw-up that sent you into a tailspin. You think you may as well give up and go back to doing things the way you did before Christ called you.

Know this: God is never shocked by your failures. Jesus knew about Peter's denial before it ever happened. When Christ called you, He knew about all your future sins and all your weaknesses, but *He called you anyway.* God can restore you to your calling just like we see Him restore Peter.

Peter, and the disciples with him, had fished all night and caught nothing. But at a suggestion from a voice on the distant shore, they cast the net on the other side of the boat. The catch was so large, they couldn't haul it in.

John then realized that the voice on the shore was Jesus, and at his announcement, Peter threw himself into the water and *swam* to Jesus.

This. *This* is what we should do when we sin! Peter couldn't get to Jesus fast enough! Can't you feel his elation at seeing the Lord—the desperation to be reunited with Him? No matter how great or small, every time we fail, we should run *toward* Him instead of away.

And don't you think Jesus's actions here harken back to Peter's initial calling? Yet another time they'd fished all night and caught nothing, but "at His word," they went out again and caught so much their nets broke.

Peter had failed, yet here was Jesus coming after him, renewing the sense of awe and wonder that had first drawn him—restoring the joy of his salvation.[71]

Satan wants you to flounder in guilt and shame. He wants you to run from Christ, go back to your old ways, and give up your calling.

But Jesus wants you to repent and come running back…or swimming back, if that's what it takes.

Watch how gently Jesus reaffirmed Peter's commitment. No harsh words or reprimands—just, "Do you love Me?"

"*Yes!* You know I do!" Peter answered.

Not once or twice, but three times Jesus asked, and Peter answered. Three times, he had disavowed Jesus; now three times, he affirmed his love. It's an undoing—a reversal of Peter's failure.

This affirmation was not for Jesus's sake, but for Peter's. Focusing on yourself and your failures directs you away from God, but focusing on your love for Him is a renewal—a fresh commitment and a reminder of the object of your faith. It stops your inward spiral and puts the spotlight back on Christ where it belongs.

When we fail, we often think of ways to try to punish ourselves. Somehow, it makes us feel better to be miserable for some undetermined amount of time. But any miserable feeling that sends us away from God is not godly. It is us hiding in our shame. For "godly grief produces a repentance that leads to salvation without regret, whereas worldly grief produces death."[72]

---

71   Psalm 51:12
72   2 Corinthians 7:10

If you find yourself ruminating on your failure and abandoning God's call and fellowship, that is worldly grief arising out of self-pity and pride, not the godly grief that leads to humility, repentance, and a glorious reunion with Him.

It isn't penance and punishment Jesus asks for; it's repentance and a return to Him. There's no amount of feeling sufficiently guilty—no mortification or punishment you can put on yourself that makes up for your failing. Jesus is our advocate—our defender before the throne.[73] Only Jesus can cover your sin, and if you trust Him as your Savior, *He already has.*

None of our sins—not the ones before *or after* we come to Christ—are too big for Him. Jesus's sacrifice atones for them all. He does not want your shame and regret; He only wants your repentance and love.

Finally, after Peter thrice declared his love, Jesus gave a command: "Feed my sheep."

And through this command, Peter again heard the echo of his initial calling. Jesus still wanted him to be a "fisher of men" despite his failings.

It's no mistake that Jesus asked for love before giving a command. He knows that love—not fear or guilt or regret—leads to obedience. "If you love Me, you will keep My commandments."[74]

So maybe you failed your convictions, and now you're running from God because you know you messed up. You couldn't stand to look at Him, so you walked away. You grieved. You left the idea of doing anything meaningful for Him behind, because you clearly don't have what it takes.

But just like Jesus sought Peter out while he was wallowing in his failure, Christ is reaching out to you in yours. You thought

---

73 I John 2:1
74 John 14:15

He wouldn't want you anymore, but there He is. The Messiah is waiting for you on the shore!

Don't wait. Whether you run, swim, or crawl, do whatever it takes to reach Him as fast as you can. The Restorer awaits.

TAKEAWAYS:
- God is never surprised by your failure. He loves you and called you knowing all your faults and failings—past and future.
- Godly grief over your sin leads to repentance and salvation; worldly grief leads to regret and death.
- Only Jesus is able to redeem your wrongs. Attempting to punish yourself is just what the devil wants.
- It's not punishment and penance Christ wants, but love and repentance.
- Your sins should send you running toward Christ as fast as you can go, not away from Him.
- Jesus is always pursuing you and eagerly awaiting your return.

SUFFERING, PERSECUTION, AND OTHER GENERALLY HARD THINGS

> *When you suffer and lose, that does not mean you are being disobedient to God. In fact, it might mean you're right in the center of His will. The path of obedience is often marked by times of suffering and loss.*
>
> Chuck Swindoll

Why do we suffer? Why does a good God allow bad things to happen? These are age-old questions about which better minds than mine have written millions of words over millennia. I could never hope to plumb the depths of suffering in a chapter.

But I know a few things.

Number one thing I know is that I don't like it. There. I said it. I'd rather live out the rest of my life in comfortable ease than face difficulty, loss, and pain.

But I also know that's not biblical and that anyone who falls prey to the false doctrine of the "prosperity gospel" is in for a rude awakening, because Christianity is not a recipe for easy living.

Honestly, part of the reason I started writing this book is because I realized I'd let a sliver of that doctrine slip into my heart. I was mad at God for not giving me any easy seasons. It seemed like every time one difficulty ended, another began, and I'd had enough! I wanted to relax, kick my feet up, and coast. I deserved it! I'd been working hard and trying to serve Him!

We've largely come to see difficulty as a punishment, and I guess it's not surprising we feel this way. From childhood, it's drilled into us that good behavior begets positive rewards and bad behavior is punished. When things don't work this way, we feel the rules have been broken. It's not fair! We want the good guys to be rewarded and the bad guys to get justice.

Karma.

What goes around comes around.

But this is a worldly idea with worldly roots, and truth be told, we only like it when it's directed at someone else. If you believe the Gospel, you've already turned the idea of karma on its head. Christ's crucifixion ensures that we don't get the punishment we so justly deserve, and by grace, gives all others the same opportunity.

So, what is suffering doing? And can you learn to like it? *Should* you learn to like it?

Several years ago, I was sitting in church when God spoke to me and said, "Are you being buried or planted?" I know it was Him, because it had nothing to do with the sermon, and I wasn't thinking about being buried or planted either one.

That's when I realized that being buried and being planted would feel *exactly the same*. The seed wouldn't know the difference. Growth, it turns out, is messy and lonely and painful.

I hadn't ever seen anything about being buried vs. being planted when this happened, but I have come across the idea several times since, and it's always a needed reminder. It seems like half my Christian walk is spent re-learning lessons, because I still have trouble being joyful and trusting God when the dirt is piling on and I find myself alone in the dank, dark mud.

It's human nature to view any trial as an impediment to what God wants to do in your life—a sign that He's not working—but nothing could be further from the truth. Your greatest triumph often arises out of your greatest affliction.

You may never know exactly what fruit God will bring out of your pain, but you can be confident that your sufferings are not wasted. God says so: "...for those who love God all things work together for good, for those who are called according to His purpose."[75]

All things.

You are *planted* (not buried!)...

...when you lose your job and don't know how you'll feed your family.

...when your spouse has been unfaithful.

...when your parents don't remember who you are.

...when your child is terminally ill.

...when war and violence threaten the safety of you and your loved ones.

God is the God of transformation, and all your sufferings will become something beautiful. As Christians, our burial—our suffering—is *always* a planting. "Truly, truly, I say to you, unless a grain of wheat falls into the earth and dies, it remains alone; but if it dies, it bears much fruit."[76]

There are so many biblical examples of this!

In Acts 16, Paul and Silas were arrested, stripped, beaten with rods, imprisoned, and put in stocks.

---

75 Romans 8:28
76 John 12:24

It's easy for us to pass over these words without thinking about what that would've actually been like. They were human, just like you and me. Imagine if you were:

...*arrested.*
...*stripped.*
...*beaten with rods.*
...*imprisoned.*
...*chained.*

And all when you'd done nothing wrong. Paul and Silas could have been in fearful hysterics, wallowing in self-pity, or angry with God. They were doing His work after all!

Instead, they *sang.* They sang, and they prayed.

If this happened to me, I'm sure my reaction would be some combination of horror, fear, confusion, and anger. Based on my level of indignance at the slightest injustice, I'm afraid I wouldn't be singing.

Naked, in pain, and chained in the innermost prison, don't you think they *felt* buried?

But they *knew* they were planted. They knew it so fully that even when the earthquake came and loosed their chains and opened the prison doors, they trusted God and did not flee. The miraculous rescue was not designed so Paul and Silas could escape, but so the jailer and all his household would come to salvation because of their decision not to.

Clearly guided by the Holy Spirit, Paul and Silas did not take their chance of escape just as Jesus did not take Himself down from the cross, and their willing submission to suffering drew others to Christ. They couldn't have known what fruit their sacrifice would produce, but Paul later writes of his suffering: "I endure everything for the sake of the elect, that they also may obtain the salvation that is in Christ Jesus with eternal glory."[77] He understood that God transforms suffering into salvation.

Joseph's suffering, too, brought about the physical salvation of entire nations during the famine. Had he not been betrayed, sold into slavery, imprisoned, falsely accused, and forgotten, countless lives would have been lost in starvation. What Joseph's brothers meant for evil, God meant for good.[78]

Even our own glorious redemption from sin—the greatest triumph of all time—came from Jesus's torture, death, and burial. His highest purpose was fulfilled in His torment—once again, *suffering into salvation.*

With the example of Christ Himself, sinless and perfect as He was, it should be clear that not all suffering is a punishment, but it's a common enough assumption, made by both Job's friends and the disciples.

Job's friends tried to tell him if he would only repent, God would restore him. They were certain his sufferings were due to some misstep on his part, but the Lord rebuked them. God wanted us to know that repentance isn't a magic wand you wave in exchange for an easy life and that there are higher purposes for our pain.

The disciples asked, "'Rabbi, who sinned, this man or his parents, that he was born blind?' Jesus answered, 'It was not that this man sinned, or his parents, but that the works of God might be displayed in him.'"[79]

And suffering is not only for the good of others. It also changes *you.*

"Since therefore Christ suffered in the flesh, arm yourselves with the same way of thinking, for whoever has suffered in the

---

[77] 2 Timothy 2:10
[78] Genesis 50:20
[79] John 9:2-3

flesh has ceased from sin, so as to live for the rest of the time in the flesh no longer for human passions but for the will of God."[80]

Trials and pain have a way of clarifying truth, bringing perspective, and turning our focus away from the earthly—the temporary—to the eternal where our hope *should* lie.

I already mentioned this Bible verse in the chapter on self-sufficiency, but it's too good not to use again: "we rejoice in our sufferings, knowing that suffering produces endurance, and endurance produces character, and character produces hope...."[81]

Haven't you seen the cancer patient who begins living with more joy than ever before? The widow filled with Christ's love and caring for those around her in the midst of her grief?

Those who have lived lives full of sorrow and pain have a clarity about what really matters.

Suffering is the intense pressure that creates the diamond, the pruning shears that make the flowers grow, the refining fire that burns away the dross of this world and helps to cast off the fleeting, fleshly things that too often take your eyes away from God. As your earthly life diminishes, the heavenly, eternal things become clearer, and your faith is transformed from something murky and shifting and common to being something solid and shining and beautiful. It solidifies into a peace and hope the world doesn't understand, but that they see and desire.

George Mueller was a 19th century evangelist and model of faith who ran several orphanages impacting the lives of over ten-thousand children. (His autobiography is a must-read, by the way.) Someone asked him how to have a strong faith, and Mueller answered: "The only way to learn strong faith is to endure great trials. I have learned my faith by standing firm amid severe testings."

---

80 I Peter 4:1
81 Romans 5:3-4

Wasn't the faith of the blind man sealed when God healed his blindness? Wasn't the faith of the disciples grown when Jesus calmed the storm that threatened to overturn the boat? Would Elijah have trusted so fully if he had never been starving in the desert and fed by ravens and from an oil jar that never ran dry?

How would we ever see God's power if we had no need for it? And where would the need for it arise if there were not trials?

If God's protection and blessing surrounds us at every moment, wouldn't it be terribly easy to place our faith in the gift rather than the Giver?

That was, after all, the accusation Satan leveled at Job. Some people will never believe your faith is real until God is all you have left. I definitely do not mean this to cheapen the faith of those who have not faced great struggles. Those people can have a genuine, life-giving relationship with God, too. But the world often sees it this way, so when they watch you continue in faith and hope despite pain and grief and injustice, the Gospel will be shining through more brightly than ever. People will ask, "Why do they carry on? Why do they still trust? What is this hope that they have?"

Your response to suffering and hardship may be your greatest opportunity to be a witness to those around you. But what does that look like? How do you "rejoice in your sufferings?"

I think a lot of Christians understand it to mean you have to fake it and pretend all is well.

I'm fine! Nothing bothers me!

I don't think that's biblical. "There is a time to weep and a time to laugh, a time to mourn and a time to dance,"[82] after all.

Nobody *likes* suffering. Even Jesus prayed, "If it be possible, let this cup pass from Me."[83]

[82] Ecclesiastes 3:4
[83] Matthew 26:39

Like Job, it's OK to ask, "Why, Lord?"[84] Like Jesus, it's OK to cry out, "My God, my God, why have You forsaken me?"[85]

The key is how they went on:

"Though He slay me, I will hope in Him."[86]

"Nevertheless, not as I will, but as You will."[87]

Facing suffering biblically doesn't look like a plastered-on smile.

It looks like contentment: "For the sake of Christ, then, I am content with weaknesses, insults, hardships, persecutions, and calamities. For when I am weak, then I am strong."[88]

It looks like trusting God's promises while continuing in His work: "…let those who suffer according to God's will entrust their souls to a faithful Creator while doing good."[89]

It looks like reacting to injustice with love and undeserved generosity: "Do not resist the one who is evil. But if anyone slaps you on the right cheek, turn to him the other also. And if anyone would sue you and take your tunic, let him have your cloak as well. And if anyone forces you to go one mile, go with him two miles."[90]

It looks like putting our hope in eternity rather than the things of this earth: "…you joyfully accepted the plundering of your property, since you knew that you yourselves had a better possession and an abiding one."[91]

It looks like holding fast to God's love and care even when our lives are threatened: "…do not fear those who kill the body but cannot kill the soul. Rather fear Him who can destroy both soul

---

84 Job 7:20
85 Matt 27:46
86 Job 13:15
87 Matthew 26:39
88 2 Corinthians 12:10
89 I Peter 4:19
90 Matthew 5:39-41
91 Hebrews 10:34

and body in hell. Are not two sparrows sold for a penny? And not one of them will fall to the ground apart from your Father."[92]

It looks like not insulting when we are insulted and not threatening when we are abused.[93]

It looks like patience: "…be patient in tribulation."[94]

It looks like responding to evil men with kindness and respect: "Repay no one evil for evil, but give thought to do what is honorable in the sight of all."[95]

It looks like being afflicted, but not crushed, perplexed, but not driven to despair, persecuted, but not forsaken, struck down, but not destroyed.[96]

This sounds hard. It IS hard. In this world, it often looks like the bad guy wins. But we should "not grow weary of doing good, for in due season we will reap, if we do not give up."[97] We will reap, and so will they: "Fret not yourself because of evildoers; be not envious of wrongdoers. For they will soon fade like the grass and wither like the green herb."[98] It's not our job to worry about that, for "Vengeance is mine, I will repay, says the Lord."[99] Our job is, "If possible, so far as it depends on us, to live peaceably with all, and never avenge ourselves, but leave the wrath to God."[100]

You will not win everyone over to salvation or even friendship. Just as the world hated and rejected Jesus, it may hate and reject you. But we have a chance to reach those whose hearts are ready, and in doing so even in the midst of insult and injury, we will be following Christ's example.

92   Matthew 10:28-29
93   I Peter 2:23
94   Romans 12:12
95   Romans 12:17
96   2 Corinthians 4:8
97   Galatians 6:9
98   Psalm 37:1
99   Romans 12:19
100 Romans 12:18-19

SUFFERING, PERSECUTION, AND OTHER GENERALLY HARD THINGS

And to be clear, I'm not only talking about persecution arising from living out your faith. I'm also talking about the everyday trials and difficulties that come from living in this fallen world—the "rain that falls on the just and the unjust alike,"[101] in other words—grief, illness, anger, rude people, insurance snafus, and being cut off in traffic. Some of those may not qualify as suffering, but they are a testing of our faith, and people watch how we respond.

"Count it all joy, my brothers, when you meet trials of various kinds, for you know that the testing of your faith produces steadfastness."[102]

"In this you rejoice, though now for a little while, if necessary, you have been grieved by various trials, so that the tested genuineness of your faith—more precious than gold that perishes though it is tested by fire—may be found to result in praise and glory and honor at the revelation of Jesus Christ."[103]

Without struggle, suffering, persecution, and other "various trials," our faith seems naïve and easy to those in the world. As in fiction, the more there is to overcome, the more powerful the story. If Frodo had simply to toss the ring of power into his hearthfire to destroy it, we would not care. It's because we watch him carry a burden he never wanted through pain and heartache and danger and betrayal and hunger and depression and loneliness that we love him and are inspired. We watch him endure, because we want to know that we can endure, too.

That is what we, as Christians, should be to the world, and this dialogue from *Lord of the Rings: The Two Towers* movie captures it in better words than I ever could:

---

101 Matthew 5:45
102 James 1:2-3
103 I Peter 1:6-7

Sam: "It's like in the great stories, Mr. Frodo. The ones that really mattered. Full of darkness and danger, they were. And sometimes you didn't want to know the end. Because how could the end be happy? How could the world go back to the way it was when so much bad had happened? But in the end, it's only a passing thing, this shadow. Even darkness must pass. A new day will come. And when the sun shines, it will shine out the clearer. Those were the stories that stayed with you—that meant something, even if you were too small to understand why. But I think, Mr. Frodo, I do understand. I know now. Folk in those stories had lots of chances of turning back, only they didn't. They kept going. Because they were holding on to something."

Frodo: "What are we holding onto, Sam?"

Sam: "That there's some good in this world, Mr. Frodo...and it's worth fighting for."

That's a beautiful passage, and Sam is mostly right. But we, as Christians, are holding on to something far bigger than the good in *this* world. We're holding on to the ultimate good beyond this world—the source of all hope, the perfect Creator, the embodiment of everything true in the universe—past, present, and future.

This is why we can hope—why we can carry on in faith.

The world *wants* to know how to carry on. If we could only see our stories from the Author's perspective and know the evil we hold at bay with our steps of faith, no matter how fearful and faltering they are, we would never turn back, never give up.

All our sufferings shine with purpose. God turns mourning into dancing,[104] ashes into beauty,[105] death into victory,[106] and suffering into salvation.

We are living the "Great Story" for all the world to see. People want to overcome, and we can show them how: "For everyone who has been born of God overcomes the world. And this is the victory that has overcome the world—our faith. Who is it that overcomes the world except the one who believes that Jesus is the Son of God?"[107]

If we could put our worst earthly agonies on one side of a scale, and the wonderful infinity we will live with Christ on the other, the pain wouldn't even register. Paul says exactly this: "For I consider that the sufferings of this present time are not worth comparing with the glory that is to be revealed to us."[108] And he repeats it here: "For this light, momentary affliction is preparing for us an eternal weight of glory beyond all comparison as we look not to the things that are seen but to the things that are unseen. For the things that are seen are transient, but the things that are unseen are eternal."[109]

And isn't that worth carrying our burdens hopefully and pressing on through danger and betrayal and pain?

---

104   Psalm 30:11
105   Isaiah 61:3
106   I Corinthians 15:55-57
107   I John 5:4
108   Romans 8:18
109   2 Corinthians 4:17-18

TAKEAWAYS:
- Suffering *feels* like being buried, but as Christians, God's promise tells us it is a planting that will yield good fruit in the end.
- Suffering and hardship do NOT mean you are outside of God's will.
- God often transforms your suffering into salvation.
- Suffering and trials are not always a punishment.
- Hardship shifts your perspective from the earthly to the eternal.
- Suffering transforms you and your faith into something beautiful, shining a light on your faith in a way nothing else can.
- Some people will never believe your faith is real until they see you in times of trouble.
- Suffering may present you with your best opportunity to be a witness to those around you.
- Rejoicing in your suffering doesn't mean you have to pretend to like it. You can mourn, yet still live in contentment, hope, faith, and love.
- The world needs to see you suffer and endure difficulty well. They need the eternal hope you have in Christ, and your example of faith is more powerful than ever when you have every earthly reason to give up.

DISTRACTION

You will never reach your destination if you stop and throw stones at every dog that barks.

Winston S. Churchill

Distraction is a thief, and when I give in to it, I'm an accomplice to the crime.

I know that sounds harsh. No one would say distraction is a *good* thing, but it seems innocuous when you stick it in a list of infamous sins. That's why it's so dangerous. It's *sneaky*.

It steals time I could be spending sitting at the Lord's feet or working on what He has called me to do for His Kingdom and ensures I don't accomplish the things I would say are most important to me.

While living distracted lives, we might bustle around doing all sorts of "useful" things without ever actually getting to the real stuff—the *important* stuff. Distraction makes us slaves to other people's expectations and phone calls and social media and the next urgent thing that pops up.

My friend needed me.
The dishes were piled up.
The mailman brought a slew of paperwork.

On and on and on, the day dwindles away. We're doing *things*, sure. But somehow, when our heads hit the pillow, we're left with the nagging feeling we've done nothing at all.

But I had to do that stuff, we think. I really did need to do the dishes, and my friend really was in crisis, and so on and so forth. So, we barrel on, trying not to think about whether we're accomplishing anything worthwhile.

You don't have to live this way. God didn't put you (or me!) here to play a giant game of whack-a-mole, frantically attending to everything that pops up in front of you. He told us to "number our days"[110] because we aren't guaranteed tomorrow.[111] He told us to "make the best use of our time."[112] We should be living with intention, purpose, and guidance from the Holy Spirit.

I really struggle with distraction. I am a to-do-list-checking, notification-clearing junkie. I want the laundry done, the bushes trimmed, the emails cleared, the comments acknowledged, and the paperwork complete.

Then I'll write, I tell myself.

But that's a lie, because the work is *never* complete. And when I allow my task list to control my time instead of being intentional with it, I'm too mentally exhausted to bring my best to anything else.

Like a car running over nail after nail spilled on the highway, I might keep coasting for a little while, but eventually, I'll crash and burn, tires flat and unable to reach my destination.

It might not be writing for you. It may be learning a language so you can minister to a marginalized people in your area, coordinating the homeless outreach for your church, or pouring time into your children. Whatever it is, God called us all to share His

---

110   Psalm 90:12
111   James 4:14
112   Colossians 4:5 and Ephesians 5:16

love with others in such a way that they are drawn closer to Him. He has kingdom work for us—work with eternity in mind.

That looks different for everyone, but it will always require dedication and effort, and if you don't make it a priority, it will fall by the wayside. It's always the significant things that get put off, because we think we can do them *later*. But later is a lie that will prevent you from ever stepping forward into the most important work.

So, how do you know where to put your time and priorities? Shouldn't we help people when they need help and attend to our responsibilities? The wonderfully ambiguous answer is, "Yes, but…

…maybe not right now."

…maybe not in the way you think."

…maybe it's not even your responsibility."

If Jesus is our primary example (and He is), then we can see He did not respond to others' expectations, demands, or even emergencies in the way we might expect.

The most stirring example of this is Lazarus's illness and death in John 11. When Jesus received word that Lazarus—"the one whom he loved"—was sick, He continued teaching where He was for *two more days*.

Imagine if your loved one were seriously ill, and you *knew* you could heal him. Wouldn't your natural reaction be to run to his aid as quickly as possible? If you didn't, everyone would think you didn't care—didn't actually love him at all.

Don't you think that's what Lazarus's sister Mary felt when she fell, weeping, at Jesus's feet and cried, "Lord, if You had been here, my brother would not have died?"[113]

---

[113] John 11:32

You could have stopped this. Why didn't You come? We thought You loved him!

Though Jesus didn't allow the emergency nor other people's expectations to affect His *actions*, that doesn't mean *He* was unaffected. Arriving after Lazarus's death, He was "deeply moved" and "greatly troubled" by Mary's grief, and He wept as He inquired about Lazarus's tomb.[114]

Jesus's decision to wait was determined by His intimate fellowship with the Father. He understood what would bring the greatest glory to God. Since you and I can't read the future, we must trust these kinds of decisions to the guidance of the Holy Spirit. That's why we must "seek first the Kingdom of God"[115] and "pray without ceasing."[116] If we're not doing that, all we have is common sense, and every situation does not call for the reaction our common sense would demand.

In Mark 1:35, we see Jesus rise early in the morning while it was still dark to go pray in a "desolate place." I don't know how long He was out there, but it was long enough that the crowds expecting Him grew restless. Jesus had been teaching and healing and casting out demons, and throngs of excited people wanted to see more, but He knew that time with His Father was the priority.

The disciples finally found Him and said, "Everyone is looking for you!"

But Jesus answered, "Let us go on to the next towns, that I may preach there also, for that is why I came out."[117]

Can you imagine the disciples' dismay? It's pretty bad PR. All those people were expecting Jesus, and He just wanted to move on to the next town without a word! He didn't want to go back and

---

114 John 11:33-35
115 Matthew 6:33
116 I Thessalonians 5:17
117 Mark 1:37-38

make an announcement, apologize diplomatically for His disappearance, or invite the crowds to follow Him to the next city. He wasn't worried about disappointing people, because He knew that God's guidance trumps man's expectation. He simply sought the Father's voice and followed it.

This is the same contrast we see between Mary and Martha in Luke 10.

"Now as they went on their way, Jesus entered a village. And a woman named Martha welcomed Him into her house. And she had a sister called Mary, who sat at the Lord's feet and listened to His teaching. But Martha was distracted with much serving. And she went up to Him and said, 'Lord, do You not care that my sister has left me to serve alone? Tell her then to help me.' But the Lord answered her, 'Martha, Martha, you are anxious and troubled about many things, but one thing is necessary. Mary has chosen the good portion, which will not be taken away from her.'"[118]

Like Martha, we are often "distracted with much serving" and "anxious and troubled about many things." We forget to ask God if this is the service He wants us to be doing. We rush from labor to labor, but it feels empty, and we begin to resent the responsibility.

But when I read this story—and I read it often, because I need frequent reminders—I breathe a sigh of relief. I don't *have* to do all the things. That's not a burden the Lord placed on me. That's a burden I place on myself.

Martha decided on her own how best to serve Jesus. She felt burdened and embittered by it, and it wasn't even what He wanted. If you are feeling pressured and stressed by doing the Lord's work, I would challenge you to step back and ask if this is a task God really asked of you or a task you put upon yourself.

[118] Luke 10:38-42

God only wants us to do *one* thing—to choose "the good portion." He wants us to live in His presence. "Come to Me, all who labor and are heavy laden, and I will give you rest."[119] Everything else He calls us to will flow from His endless fountain of living water. Our strength will be renewed, and we will mount up with wings like eagles. We will be able to run and not grow weary, walk and not faint.[120]

That doesn't necessarily mean what God asks of us will be easy. But when I find my fruits of the Spirit are buried under resentment and emotional exhaustion, it's a sure sign I'm either working on the wrong things or I haven't spent enough time sitting at the feet of Jesus. Normally, it means both.

There is clearly a time to work and go to the aid of others. There are verses upon verses instructing us to work diligently and to serve one another. If we follow Jesus's example and the thread of Ecclesiastes 3, there is a time to do dishes and a time to leave them, a time to answer the phone and a time to let it ring, a time to mow the yard and a time to not care if your neighbors are mad at you, a time to hasten to your brother's aid and a time to stay where you are.

And if that's the case, how can we ever know the difference if we are not walking daily in God's presence?

We want a clear, black-and-white decision—"if X, then Y"—a formula that works every time.

But that's not a relationship, that's math.

Our default is to choose our actions based on what makes sense, but what made sense when Jesus received word that Lazarus was ill would have been for Him to run as fast as He could to heal "him who He loved." But that would have robbed God of glory.

[119] Matthew 11:28
[120] Isaiah 40:31

What made sense in Mark 1 would have been for Jesus to go back to those crowds expecting Him and serve more, heal more, teach more, build up more excitement for His "movement," and gather more "fans." I say it that way because if that's what He had chosen, that's all He would've been doing—building fans for a movement.

And that's the risk we run if we depend only on our logic instead of seeking the Lord's guidance as well. If we are not sitting at His feet, hearing His word, and following where He leads, all the service in the world will count for nothing in the end but wood, hay, and stubble. "For no one can lay a foundation other than that which is laid, which is Jesus Christ. Now if anyone builds on the foundation with gold, silver, precious stones, wood, hay, straw—each one's work will become manifest, for the Day will disclose it, because it will be revealed by fire, and the fire will test what sort of work each one has done. If the work that anyone has built on the foundation survives, he will receive a reward."[121]

In *My Utmost for His Highest,* Oswald Chambers says, "Beware of anything that competes with loyalty to Jesus Christ. The greatest competitor of devotion to Jesus is service for Him."[122]

I'm afraid much of my busyness for God is only that—busyness. It is easier to serve God where it makes sense to me than it is to listen, and all my well-meaning, but fruitless activity will be burned up in the end.

When you settle in to do the important kingdom work God has for you, suddenly everything else in the world will seem more important. It will feel imperative that you make that phone call, do the yardwork, pay the bills, order your kid's soccer uniform, or

---

121 I Corinthians 3:11-14
122 Taken from *My Utmost for His Highest* by Oswald Chambers, © 1935 by Dodd Mead & Co., renewed © 1963 by the Oswald Chambers Publications Assn., Ltd. Used by permission of Our Daily Bread Publishing, Grand Rapids, MI 49501. All rights reserved.

touch base with that contact you met at a networking meeting last month. It's all too easy to convince yourself that the distraction is the thing you should be doing.

But if I search my heart, I realize that much of what I'm focused on is fleshly and based on my own desires and inclinations. So many of the things that distract me from Christ are things that can wait. It's just not in my Type A nature to *like* waiting, and my preference for task-completion makes it easy for the devil to manipulate me into focusing on the urgent rather than the important. He just has to throw more projects in front of me.

Whatever means the devil uses to distract you, with each new task, you should turn to Christ and ask, "Where do you want me to put my time, Lord?"

We must train ourselves to heed the still, small voice.

The truth is when I take time to do this, the unfinished tasks on my to-do list no longer weigh on me, because I know I spent my time according to God's guidance. Instead of that uncomfortable "did-I-accomplish-anything-meaningful" feeling, I have confidence that He steered me to the work that needed to be done.

There is a balance of priorities that can only be reached by sitting long at the feet of Jesus even when—*especially* when—you think you don't have the time. We must trust God with all the disturbances and distractions that need our attention, and learn from Him where our time should be spent.

In *The Still Small Voice; Quiet Hour Talks* by G.P Pardington, he gives this idea beautiful imagery: "The troubled surface of a lake will not reflect an object. Our lives must be quiet and restful if we would see God."

Too often, like Martha, we allow ourselves to be busy in the work of this world and neglect the work of eternity. Instead of being "anxious and troubled about many things" and "distracted with much serving," we should heed the promptings of the Holy Spirit and rely on the strength and sovereignty of our God to take care of all the other unfinished tasks that swarm for our attention.

I know that telling you to sit at Jesus's feet and listen feels like nebulous advice. That's one of the reasons it's so much easier to focus on energetic service. We want something concrete. But the more time you spend in the Lord's presence, the less vague this feels—His voice becomes clearer, Scripture reaches deeper, and the Holy Spirit prompts more distinctly.

The Bible gives us so many promises that we will hear and know His voice:

"My sheep hear My voice, and I know them, and they follow Me."[123]

"Call to Me, and I will answer you, and will tell you great and hidden things that you have not known."[124]

"And your ears shall hear a word behind you, saying, 'This is the way, walk in it,' when you turn to the right or when you turn to the left."[125]

We also have the Holy Spirit:

"But the Helper, the Holy Spirit, whom the Father will send in My name, He will teach you all things and bring to your remembrance all that I have said to you."[126]

And, of course, the Bible itself:

"All Scripture is breathed out by God and profitable for teaching, for reproof, for correction, and for training in righteousness, that the man of God may be competent, equipped for every good work."[127]

---

123 John 10:27
124 Jeremiah 33:3
125 Isaiah 30:21
126 John 14:26
127 2 Timothy 3:16-17

But all of these still require that we are intimately, completely, and continually connected to God in prayer and in the Word—to be Jesus praying alone in a desolate place, to be Mary instead of Martha, sitting at His feet, drinking in His teachings instead of bustling around trying to serve Him in ways He never asked. Even if circumstances seem to demand your action or your service, take a step back and check in with the Lord.

Jesus—the sinless incarnation of God Himself—considered spending time with the Father so essential that He sneaked away to the desert to accomplish it. How much more vital is it for us, housed in these fleshly bodies and subject to the whims of our nature and the ploys of the devil?

And in this dependence on the Lord's guidance, there is a beautiful freedom from the burdens He never meant for you. Oswald Chambers says, in yet another brilliant quote from *My Utmost for His Highest*:

"Beware of any work for God which enables you to evade concentration on Him. A great many Christian workers worship their work. The one concern of a worker should be concentration on God, and this will mean that all the other margins of life, mental, moral, and spiritual, are free with the freedom of a child—a worshipping child, not a wayward child."[128]

We need no longer allow the crushing weight of responsibility to overwhelm us in spirit and in body. Our one task—the good portion—is to sit and rest at His feet. Any good work with merit will flow like rivers of living water[129] out of the abundant life[130] we draw from Him.

---

128 Taken from *My Utmost for His Highest* by Oswald Chambers, © 1935 by Dodd Mead & Co., renewed © 1963 by the Oswald Chambers Publications Assn., Ltd. Used by permission of Our Daily Bread Publishing, Grand Rapids, MI 49501. All rights reserved.
129 John 7:28
130 John 10:10

TAKEAWAYS:
- Distractions steal time from the work God has given you.
- You don't have to take care of every task or even emergency that pops up in front of you. If you try, you'll likely burn out before you ever get to the work God has for you.
- The only way to know how to spend your time is to be in constant contact with the Lord in prayer, in the Word, and listening to the Holy Spirit.
- Sometimes doing what the Lord leads means other people are disappointed and hurt by your actions.
- Sometimes you decide how Jesus wants you to serve because it makes sense, but it's not necessarily even what He wants you to be doing.
- If you're feeling bitter about the work God asked of you, it's a sure sign you need to spend more time at His feet.
- There is no formula that will tell you how to prioritize your responsibilities. That's why *relationship* is the key.
- It's easy to let service *for* Christ overtake your relationship *with* Christ.
- The devil knows your natural inclinations and will use them to distract you from the real work.
- The more time you spend with the Lord, the more clearly you will hear His voice.
- Trusting His guidance in where you apply your efforts frees you from the burden of your unfinished tasks. Even if your to-do list is still a mile long, you will know you have done the most important things.

LAZINESS

Most of us know perfectly well what we ought to do; our trouble is that we do not want to do it.

Peter Marshall

I almost didn't write this chapter. Laziness almost got squished in with distraction, because the two are, for me, often indistinguishable.

I've had every reasonable distraction pulling me away from working consistently on this book. As I'm writing this in 2020, we've had multiple house leaks and septic backups and termite damage resulting in lots of unplanned, time-consuming home repairs (many of which I did myself). One of my friends said it was like my house was playing a psychotic game of dominoes. I would begin fixing one problem only to discover another. In addition to this, my family is dealing with the difficult decisions involved with aging parents, the world is in a global pandemic, and the United States is rife with racial and political tension, riots, and violence. You could say that 2020 on the whole is playing a psychotic game of dominoes.

If I needed a word to legitimately describe this season, *distraction* could be it.

All my distraction appears quite reasonable to anyone looking on from the outside. But, you see, distraction is the laziness of the prideful. I don't want to look bad. I could spend my life doing paperwork and yardwork and home repairs, and no one would ever call me lazy, but if I'm honest, much of this has simply been laziness *disguised* as distraction.

Writing this book is hard, and my brain doesn't want to do hard things. My subconscious is actually *looking* for distractions, because it's *lazy*. (And if I know anything, it's this: if you're looking for a distraction, you will find one.) There's a little part of me that's relieved with each new responsibility, thinking, *Whew. I can't possibly work on my book right now. No one would expect me to! Right now, I have to patch that drywall and hook that sink back up and figure out how to help my parents and learn about current events.*

But if I continue using that stuff as an excuse not to do what God has asked of me, I am burying my talents—it's an act of disobedience. No one else may know it, but I would, and so would the Lord.

And before you check out and say, "Oh, I'm not talented. I can't draw or sing or paint or write, so this doesn't apply to me," let me clarify. By "talents," I don't mean anything as narrow as the common use.

You're not getting off that easy!

I'm talking about anything the Lord has given you. It might be an innate ability, a desire, a developed skill, or wealth. Anything you can do for the Kingdom of God is a talent for the purposes of this chapter. If you're like me, the Holy Spirit is always nudging you with some task, and He won't let you off the hook until you do it!

Are you an encourager? A builder? Can you make people laugh? Can you teach? Do you make people feel at ease? Are you a great cook? Do people come to you for solace? Advice? Empathy?

When God gives you something, He gives it to you so you can cultivate and grow it. In doing so, it will eventually yield spiritual fruit.

I'll admit that the Parable of the Talents in Matthew 25 always puzzled me a little. I used to think of it in terms of actual dollar investments and felt a little sorry for the last guy, who, after all, didn't squander his money away on sinful things. But one day, God sort of hit me over the head with the lesson. I suddenly realized that allowing the cares of this world to continually pull me away from what He's asked of me is the equivalent of burying my "talents."

Just as that servant was supposed to invest and grow interest, our lives are supposed to bear fruit. The Bible makes it clear that believers *will* bear good fruit.[131][132][133] We can't do that if we're side-stepping our eternal purpose to focus on the things of this world.

I'm as guilty as anyone. I've been using all those seemingly legitimate distractions as excuses to put off the task God currently has for me—to write this book, which has proven more difficult than I imagined. The first few chapters came easy, and I guess I thought the rest would, too, but everything since has been painstakingly slow. It all comes out blurry, out of order, and needing rewrite upon rewrite. I've questioned whether it's worth it.

A friend asked me why I continued if I was having so much trouble.

---

[131] John 15
[132] Matthew 7:16-20
[133] Jeremiah 17:7-8

I had to think for a minute. I started it because I was seeking change in myself, but I knew that alone wouldn't have kept me writing through the difficulty. Finally, I said, "I think it can help people. It's an act of love."

"Then love me!" she said. "Love US! Stop acting like it's about you and whether you're having a good time, and go write it. If we need this book, then give it to us!"

Ouch. But also, YES. It's not about me or whether it's easy. It's about loving. By allowing worldly things to get between me and diligent work on this book, I was not loving others.

God doesn't give us a light to hide it under a bushel or talents so we can set them up on a curio shelf and admire them, think about them, and feel a little warm and fuzzy when we talk about them. He gives them to us so they can bear fruit, and the ultimate fruit is love. Frittering away our time instead of being diligent ensures our talents are never invested.

I could do all the paperwork and all the home repairs and work all the overtime, but if I have not love, I am nothing.[134] I'm not saying that paperwork and home repairs and overtime can't be acts of love, because they most certainly can, but *for me, right now,* the act of love I'm supposed to be putting first is the writing of this book, and I've been sacrificing it to my distractions, all because studying diligently, thinking hard, digging deep, and writing consistently feels like too much effort.

Is there an act of love you're burying because it's challenging? Does not making it a priority prevent others from receiving something you should be giving?

Don't let your aversion to difficulty stop you from loving others.

134 I Corinthians 13:2

In the end, not committing to faithful stewardship in the work God asks of us makes us just as "wicked and slothful" as the servant in the parable, no matter how hard we're working in other areas.

So far, I've only focused on laziness disguised as busyness... the kind of laziness that, on the surface, allows me to keep looking pretty good to the outsider.

But here's where I admit that sometimes it's just out-and-out laziness—the slouchy, unattractive, couch-potato kind. Sometimes, my procrastination has nothing to do with misplaced priorities.

Sometimes, I just want to do what I want to do—preferably, something easy. In writing this book, I've discovered a terrible tendency to flip over to social media and begin mindlessly scrolling the minute I can't find the right word or I realize the chapter needs to be rewritten entirely—in other words, as soon as the work becomes difficult.

Instead of writing, I delay and drag it out like an eight-year-old who's supposed to be cleaning her room. If I'd just buckle down and do it, it would take half the time, but instead I loll around and dawdle dramatically. I put off the hard stuff, playing with every toy I pick up in the process.

I even *like* having a clean room...or in this case, a finished book...so, what am I doing?

The War of Art by Steven Pressfield puts it this way: "Most of us have two lives; the life we live and the unlived life within us. Between the two stands resistance.... Resistance only opposes in one direction. It obstructs movement only from a lower sphere to a higher. It kicks in when we seek to pursue a calling in the arts, launch an innovative enterprise, or evolve to a higher station morally, ethically, or spiritually."

The War of Art is not a Christian book, but Mr. Pressfield certainly exposed a spiritual truth.

You could replace the word *resistance* with either "the devil" or "laziness," and the statement would be equally true. Both would prefer that you never exhibit anything like discipline or dedication. The devil wants to keep you focused on the trivial, temporal things of this world, and laziness is undoubtedly a wildly successful tool, because it also appeals to your nature.

But good things rarely happen by accident; we have to work for them. They require action—boots on the ground. Faith without works is dead.[135]

I'm not talking about legalistic, Pharisee-rules kind of works. Real works of faith will flow naturally when you're sitting at Jesus's feet. The fruit is simply what grows when you're abiding in the Vine; it's not a list of deeds you perform.

I haven't kicked my laziness habit completely, but I keep pressing on, and here is one thing I know: when I spend the time doing what the Lord wants instead of what my flesh wants, I never regret it. It may be hard to start doing it on the front end, but I'm always happy I did. I'm even refreshed. It feels good.

The idea that leisure equals enjoyment is ingrained in our culture, but this isn't actually true. Long-term satisfaction is more likely achieved by perseverance and hard work. Time spent exerting real effort to a meaningful end is more satisfying to our souls. We need to break the mindset that difficult is the same as undesirable. In my book *The Worlds Next Door,* a character asks this when another balks at difficulty: "Someone has taught you that you can only enjoy what is easy?"

This J.R. Miller quote could be an answer to that question: "There is no burden which, if we lift it cheerfully and bear it with

---

[135] James 2:17

love in our hearts, will not become a blessing to us. God means our tasks to be our helpers; to refuse to bend our shoulders to receive a load is to decline a new opportunity for growth."[136]

God has prompted each of us to kingdom work. If you don't know what that means for you, I encourage you to sit at the Jesus's feet for a while. Spend time meditating on His Word. At some point, He will lay a task on your heart. He will ask, "Whom shall I send? And who will go for us?"

I don't know about you, but I want to be Isaiah, eagerly shouting, "Here I am; send me!"[137]

How often has He asked, and we turned away?

Not now, Lord…

…I'm too tired.

…a new season of my favorite show just came out.

…the game's on.

…I don't feel like it.

…after I finish reading my book.

Like a student hoping the teacher doesn't call on him, we refuse to meet His gaze. That's what turning away from His call does; it breaks fellowship. We don't want to be near Him when we're avoiding His work.

I think most Christians would say they want to do a mighty work for God. I know I do. But the mighty works begin as tiny steps of obedience. Everyone wants to do grand things. We're sort of arrogant that way. We like the idea of being the hero—of being known as *the person who did the thing*. The problems begin because we don't want to persevere in the hard work of the day-to-day.

The June 15th devotion of *My Utmost for His Highest* by Oswald Chambers says the following: "Drudgery is the touchstone of character. The great hindrance in spiritual life is that we will

---

136 *Glimpses Through Life's Windows: Selections from the Writings of J. R. Miller*
137 Isaiah 6:8

look for big things to do, but 'Jesus took a towel...and began to wash the disciples' feet.'"[138][139]

There are so many small promptings of the Lord. Those are easy for us to ignore, because we feel that the grubby, mundane things aren't very important. We can skip them. But "one who is faithful in a very little is also faithful in much, and one who is dishonest in a very little is also dishonest in much."[140]

If the Lord asks you to wash someone's feet or clean the church bathrooms or write a book, your obedience to that call is an exercise of faith. And your disobedience is an exercise of the flesh.

When the veil is removed in death, I believe we will marvel that we ever wanted to do anything besides serve the Lord in life. My prayer is that we will begin to see His worth *now*, deny ourselves *now*, be active in His work *now*, so that on that day, like the diligent servant in the Parable of the Talents, we will hear, "Well done, good and faithful servant. You have been faithful over a little; I will set you over much. Enter into the joy of your master."[141]

TAKEAWAYS:

- Distraction is often an excuse for avoiding the hard things God's called you to do.
- Don't simply be busy; be obedient!
- You can look industrious doing many tasks that won't matter in the end.

138 Taken from *My Utmost for His Highest* by Oswald Chambers, © 1935 by Dodd Mead & Co., renewed © 1963 by the Oswald Chambers Publications Assn., Ltd. Used by permission of Our Daily Bread Publishing, Grand Rapids, MI 49501. All rights reserved.
139 John 13:4-5
140 Luke 16:10
141 Matthew 25:23

- Your talents are any works you can do for the Kingdom of God, and *you have some*. God has called all of us to be laborers for Him.
- Don't waste your talents by burying them. They're given to us to be cultivated and bear fruit.
- Burying your gifts will hinder you from loving others, because they are meant to bless those around you. If you're not using them, you're not loving well.
- A true believer will bear good fruit, and works will always follow true faith.
- Laziness is a tool the devil uses to keep you from living a fulfilled life. It will always seek to keep you on the couch.
- Don't let the mere idea of difficulty seem undesirable to you. Most things that matter require effort, and being diligent will bring more long-term satisfaction than leisure will in the end.
- Be hard-working even in the small things. God doesn't hand us a grand quest unless we've proven faithful in the everyday grind.

HURRY

My generation is in a hurry. We want everything now, now, now! We want it to happen fast and right away, or we'll make it happen.

Nathaniel Bassey

Hurry is a sickness we have in our bones. It's contagious, and the symptoms include, but are not limited to, discontentment, irritability, poor judgment, inability to focus, and impatience.

My hurry can flare up over both the minutiae and the big picture—when I consider my ever-growing daily to-do list or when I think about what I'd like to accomplish with my life on a grander scale…and sometimes just when I'm hungry.

Being in a hurry has never made me more Christlike. Not once.

It's a greedy, grasping thing. It rears its ugly head when I don't think God is going to come through, so I push as hard and as fast as I can to do it on my own. The times I have felt the deadline looming and someone or something was standing in my way are times I look back on my behavior and cringe. I'm sure if I could see myself at those moments, I'd look something like Bilbo when he was tempted to take the ring of power back from Frodo—"a little wrinkled creature with a hungry face and bony, groping hands."[142]

When I hurry, I not only make mistakes, I make bad decisions with a bad attitude.

I don't know about you, but I can feel it in my body when hurry takes over. It's this sort of frenetic discomfort buzzing through my veins. It's not at all pleasant for me or anyone I happen to be around.

The good news is it's treatable. The bad news is the treatment is painful. It requires waiting on the Lord and trusting Him with the outcome. It requires patience. It requires waiting even when we think God is late.

Saul thought God was late. The Israelites were on the cusp of a battle, and when they saw the multitude of the Philistine's forces, they began to scatter and hide.[143] Samuel had said he would meet them to make a sacrifice to the Lord in seven days and then instruct them what to do.[144] Saul knew this would rally the troops. It would remind them that the Lord was with them and give them clear direction.

But the seven days had passed, and Samuel was not there. Saul responded with classic "I guess I have to do everything myself around here" arrogance. He did not wait for the guidance of the Lord's prophet and decided to perform the sacrifice himself. Remember that only priests were allowed to perform sacrifices. Saul's action disobeyed a clear commandment of the law, and because he attempted to circumvent the Lord, the entire kingdom was taken from him.

Yep, you read that right. This one act of disobedience is the reason God took away Saul's kingship. Sobering, isn't it?

142 *The Fellowship of the Ring* – J.R.R. Tolkien
143 I Samuel 13:6
144 I Samuel 10:8

*But Samuel **was** late*, we think. *The people **were** scattering. What was Saul supposed to do? Just…wait while the great horde of Philistines closed in on them?*

The answer none of us like is: *Yes.*

Other people being late doesn't mean you get to disobey God.

One common example of this I see in our culture is people not waiting for marriage to become sexually active. I often hear Christian women say, "Well, there aren't any good Christian men. They're all immature and won't commit to marriage." Many of the women who feel this way become sexually active because they see marriage (and its benefits) as a right they've been denied by immature Christian men being unwilling to commit.

But other people not being where we think they should be, doing what we think they should be doing, when we think they should be doing it is never an excuse for us to disobey as well, even if their slowness, immaturity, or disobedience is negatively affecting our lives.

Saul took Samuel's slowness as an excuse to disobey. He was promised a sacrifice to the Lord, and the prophet was late. If you feel the Lord promised you a spouse, but that spouse is late, it doesn't mean the rest of God's precepts go out the window. It means you continue to wait on the Lord. You continue in your peace, confidence, and hope, knowing that God is still God, and He will still come through, even when we can't see how.

And, incidentally, Ladies, I've never talked to a Christian woman who did not regret making this decision. If you're feeling frustrated and ready to give in, trust the Lord. His way is always better! Compromise will only make you more dissatisfied. Gentlemen, I don't have any empirical data for you on this, as, for obvious reasons, I don't converse with men about their sexual activity. I do know, however, that the rest stands. God's rules are always for our benefit, and if your highest aim is to follow Him, compromise will only leave you defeated and will not bring you real fulfillment.

A part of me wants to delve deeply into how singleness is not a punishment, how the Bible even says "it is good to remain single,"[145] how marriage is not something everyone is guaranteed, and how I wish our culture would stop treating marriage (or its benefits) as the pinnacle of worth and happiness. But I know this is a tangent, so I'll leave it at that.

Here are a few more lessons we should learn from Saul's actions:

Other people deserting the cause—or deserting you—doesn't mean you should panic.

Saul saw his troops disappearing, panicked, and scrambled to find a way to bring them back. Many modern churches saw young people fleeing the church and panicked as well. They drummed up new activities, new attractions, and in some cases, even new theology...or sometimes just *less* theology. I'm convinced the reactive scramble to the mass exodus from organized church actually facilitated the departure rather than mitigated it. People are hungry for real food, and instead of doubling down on truth, many churches started serving up a sort of weak tea that is good for neither flavor nor rejuvenation. What we needed was people getting more serious about following God, not people attempting to use Him as a pep rally.

That's what Saul did. He wasn't seeking God first; he just wanted to win his battle. He didn't care what God wanted. If he had, he would have waited for the rightful priest to perform the sacrifice and the instruction from the Lord that priest promised

---

[145] I Corinthians 7:8

to give. But Saul just wanted to make sure the people didn't desert the cause, so he gave them a show—a façade of the real thing.

God will rally people through our *obedience*, not through a ritual performed like some sort of magic trick. Seeking what you want at the expense of obedience to God will only bring pain.

And lastly, *being under imminent threat of failure, loss of something valuable to you, or even death, doesn't mean you should rush into action.*

Sometimes the deadline is looming, the bills are piling up, and your enemies seem to have the upper hand. Like Saul, you feel hemmed in without options, and like a cornered animal, you act rashly out of fear and desperation. You *had* to do something. There was no other way out!

Any time that is your motivation, it's not an action of God. That is an act of desperation trusting in your own sensibilities, not an act of faith in the Father.

Saul didn't see any other way to pull the troops back together, and he was willing to disobey God to make that happen. This means that 1) he didn't care if he had God as long as he had an army and 2) he was basing his confidence in victory on human strength instead of in God's providence and protection.

If there is something you're willing to disobey God in order to get, then your life is not fully committed to Him. Maybe you see a horde of threats to your happiness, wealth, or security coming over the hilltop, and you turn to workaholism or exercise or sex or drunkenness in a feverish attempt to cling to them.

It *will not work*. Only clinging to and waiting for God will bring peace and satisfaction. "It is good that one should wait quietly for the salvation of the Lord."[146] If we're supposed to wait for it, that means it's coming!

146 Lamentations 3:26

Saul gave up a kingdom by attempting to rush God. How many times have I acted in haste, afraid God wasn't going to come through, someone was going to let me down, I was going to miss an opportunity, or I was going to be overwhelmed? And how many times was that action fear-based, selfish, and ultimately, fool-hardy?

Every time.

Satan will always try to rush you. There is a story of a man who sought the counsel of George Mueller about an opportunity to further the cause of Christ. Mueller was busy and sent a message that he couldn't see the man till the next day. A message came back that the matter couldn't wait; if the decision wasn't made today, thousands of dollars might be lost. Mr. Mueller said this in his reply: "If the matter cannot wait twenty-four hours, you'd better not touch it at all. If the matter was of God, it would keep that long." By the time the man came for his appointment, he had determined the whole thing was a scam, and he was grateful for Mueller's counsel.

There is no aspect of that grasping, fearful rushing that will bring about a positive result, bring you closer to the Lord, or help you positively impact others. Oswald Chambers says this in the March 22nd devotion from *My Utmost for His Highest:* "The only test as to whether we ought to allow an emotion to have its way is to see what the outcome of the emotion will be. Push it to its logical conclusion, and if the outcome is something God would condemn, allow it no more way."[147]

Follow hurry to its logical conclusion, and you will only find pain, dissatisfaction, and emptiness. Allow it no more "way" in your life.

---

147   Taken from *My Utmost for His Highest* by Oswald Chambers, © 1935 by Dodd Mead & Co., renewed © 1963 by the Oswald Chambers Publications Assn., Ltd. Used by permission of Our Daily Bread Publishing, Grand Rapids, MI 49501. All rights reserved.

Ever heard the Christian "joke" about not praying for patience because then God will send you something you must be patient for?

Forget it.

God's not twirling his mustache and gleefully dumping troubles on our heads when we ask Him to grow us. He wants to grow us so we have the tools we need to handle what's already coming.

Pray for patience, because you're going to need it. We're *all* going to need it. We *will* have to wait for something—for lots of things, actually—throughout our lives. We will have to wait for big things and small things and petty things and desperately painful things.

And you know what? The attitude of hurry *isn't helpful.* It isn't helpful when…

…that package you ordered a month ago isn't here yet.

…you're in your forties and still longing for a spouse.

…you're running late, and your 4-yr-old insists on attempting to tie his shoes *again.*

…the prognosis isn't in yet.

…your dinner at the restaurant is taking forever.

…your house is about to be foreclosed on.

At its root, hurry is a lack of trust and contentment—"Whoever believes will not be in haste."[148] But its opposite? Peace. Confidence. Hope.

Doesn't just thinking those words make you feel better? That buzzing in my veins stills a little as I read them slowly…

Peace.

Confidence.

Hope.

[148] Isaiah 28:16

And at the end of those words…or maybe the beginning…is surrender—accepting that God knows what's best for us even if it runs counter to what we think we want, accepting that He is, indeed, sovereign, and that we, indeed, are not.

When I was a young woman, I was engaged…twice. I had hurry sickness. I wanted to do the "next thing"—to go ahead and get my life started, as I saw it. Both times, I ended up breaking it off, and I'm so grateful God woke me up before I rushed Him. I eventually married at 33, and my husband is the perfect person for me. I saw this statement once, and it utterly illustrates how I feel about him: "If I were married to someone else, I'd punch him in the face and go find you." (For the record, I don't recommend this as an actual course of action.)

I don't know what my life would've been like if I'd married someone else, but I do know what kingdom I would have given up…this uniquely wonderful marriage I have wouldn't exist. Or perhaps it would but with a few more scars on its back. I'd have given up something wonderful in the future for something mediocre now. In the July 4th devotion of *Streams in the Desert*, Lettie Cowman says, "Men would pluck their mercies green when the Lord would have them ripe." Trust that the fruit will be the sweeter for the waiting—the ripening—it requires.

If you think you've already rushed God and lost the kingdom, that does not leave you floundering outside of His will forever. Your bad decisions do not set you up on an asymptotic curve, never to intersect with your true path again. There are always consequences, yes, but repentance will always bring you back. If you're on the wrong road, you must go back. As C.S. Lewis says in *Mere Christianity*, "Going back is the quickest way on."[149]

---

149   *Mere Christianity* by C.S. Lewis © Copyright C.S. Lewis Pte Ltd 1942, 1943, 1944, 1952. Extract reprinted by permission.

It's like climbing an infinite tree. If you go off the main trunk, eventually, that branch will end, you will realize you've taken a wrong turn, and you will have to go back—in other words, repent.

The tragedy of Saul is not that he lost his kingdom, but that he never repented of this transgression. He spent the rest of his life trying to regain and keep that kingdom instead of turning back to obedience. He wanted it more than he wanted to be in fellowship with God. I can't say whether he absolutely turned his back on God or not; there's no way I could know that, but we certainly never see him act like he wanted to follow God again.

But *you* can go back. If you've gone the wrong way, you may have lost something, but don't let it be the most important thing. "For what will it profit a man if he gains the whole world and forfeits his soul?"[150]

I want to make it clear that by saying "go back," I don't necessarily mean "undo." For instance, if I had married someone else, I don't think the biblical response would have been to divorce them just because I decided they weren't right for me. The biblical fix would've been to continue living a godly life as a godly wife to the best of my ability in those circumstances. Saul's biblical repentance would have been to accept the consequences of his actions, but turn back to the Lord and complete his reign—finish the race—in obedience.

As we've seen in other chapters, God can and *does* redeem our bad decisions. His mercies are new every morning.[151]

It's so much easier to get on the wrong road when you're in a hurry, speeding along, and not taking time to consult the directions. God is your GPS, but He can only guide you if you have

150 Mark 8:36
151 Lamentations 3:22-23

the Wi-Fi on and the volume up. Rest, listen, and obey, and He will not lead you astray.

There are so many verses about waiting on the Lord. I did a study on it once, because I felt like I needed the lesson. And did you know that at least two of the most common Hebrew words used for "wait" in the Bible—*qavah* and *yachal*—are both interchangeable with the word "hope?"

If we're waiting on the Lord, it also means that we are hoping in Him instead of our own understanding,[152] instead of chariots and horses,[153] instead of the stores we have filling up our barns.[154]

Don't rush God, but "commit your way to the Lord, trust in Him, and He will act."[155]

God is never late.

TAKEAWAYS:

- Hurry does not make you more Christlike.
- Hurry is a sickness, and the cure is patience and trust.
- Other people being late or slow from disobedience or immaturity doesn't mean you get to disobey God, even when their actions seem to be hurting your outcome.
- A mad scramble to cling to some earthly desire you're scared to lose is not trusting God—even when that earthly desire is your survival.
- Only clinging to God will bring about ultimate satisfaction.
- Yes! Pray for patience!

---

152   Proverbs 3:5
153   Psalm 20:7
154   Luke 12:16-21
155   Psalm 37:5

- If you fight for something that's outside of God's will, you may be missing the bigger blessing He was holding for you.
- If you've rushed God, you're not "one and done." The Lord's mercies are new every morning, and He will direct your steps from that point forward any time you choose Him.
- The word "wait" in Hebrew is interchangeable with the word "hope." When you wait, you are placing your hope on the firm foundation rather than the sinking sands of this world.
- God is never late, nor is He early! He's always precisely on time.

PROSPERITY

Prosperity knits a man to the world. He feels that he is 'finding his place in it,' while really, it is finding its place in him. His increasing reputation, his widening circle of acquaintances, his sense of importance, the growing pressure of absorbing and agreeable work, build up in him a sense of being really at home in earth.[156]

C.S. Lewis, *The Screwtape Letters*

I used to have that quote taped to my mirror where I could see it every day. It helped me remember that maybe finding my place in the world wasn't all it was cracked up to be. "Losing my place" became a sort of mantra I would say when I felt like the world didn't want me and my life wasn't working out the way I wanted it to.

It was comforting. It still is.

However, I have to admit that the human side of me has never stopped striving to find my place. I want a comfortable living with nice things, relationships that bring me joy, and work that I find meaningful.

---

[156] *The Screwtape Letters* by C.S. Lewis © Copyright C.S. Lewis Pte Ltd 1942. Extract reprinted by permission.

In other words, I still want to feel at home on this earth. I don't think it's inherently wrong to hope for good things even in the here and now, but when the pursuit of *this* home gets in the way of the pursuit of our *real* home, it is. And it often does.

The more stuff and the more connections we have luring us into thinking we can have heaven on earth, the more difficult it becomes to fix our eyes on Jesus[157] and prioritize eternal things.[158]

Consider the perfect candidate for Christendom: the rich young ruler.

This young man ran up and knelt before Jesus. "Good Teacher, what must I do to inherit eternal life?"[159]

This was a great start. He clearly didn't want to miss the good news. He knelt to honor Jesus and called Him teacher.

But Jesus knew the guy's heart and didn't pull any punches. Jesus answered, "'You lack one thing: go, sell all that you have and give to the poor, and you will have treasure in Heaven; and come, follow Me.' Disheartened by the saying, he went away sorrowful, for he had great possessions."[160]

This sounds harsh to us. We don't really get it. Jesus didn't ask this of all His disciples, so why did He ask it of this young man?

Because Jesus knew wealth was this guy's hang-up—the one earthly thing he could not turn away from. The guy was sad about it, sure, but his actions said, "I'm not willing to give that up. I have more faith in my money than I have in You. I want my wealth more than I want eternal life—more than I want You."

The rich young ruler wanted to believe God with his words, but he wasn't willing to put his money where his mouth was. He wanted to make trusting God an intellectual exercise or may-

---

157 Hebrews 12:2
158 2 Corinthians 4:18
159 Mark 10:17
160 Mark 10:21-22

be another rule he could follow—not something that radically changed his life. He wanted the good life with a little Jesus on top.

But Jesus isn't something extra you use to flavor your meal. Jesus is *dinner*. He is nourishment and bread—the hearty brown kind, dense and full of flavor. He tells us: "I am the Bread of Life; whoever comes to Me shall not hunger, and whoever believes in Me shall never thirst."[161]

After the young man has gone, Jesus says to His disciples, "Truly, I say to you, there is no one who has left house or brothers or sisters or mother or father or children or lands, for my sake and for the gospel, who will not receive a hundredfold now in this time, houses and brothers and sisters and mothers and children and lands, with persecutions, and in the age to come, eternal life."[162]

Whatever you struggle to give up, God wants to give you something more. Do we really believe that? It doesn't seem so, or we wouldn't clench our fists in fear and stubbornness, crying out, *Not that, Lord!*

Not my comfortable house!

Not my sexuality!

Not my hopes for marriage and children!

Not my career!

When I started this book, I had an unfulfilled desire that was crushing my soul and coming between me and Christ. It was a desire for ease. *I paid my dues,* I thought. *I've been working hard my whole life. It's time for easy.*

I was mad that God wasn't giving it. See, I thought I was finally there. I'd sold my cleaning business to start doing the administrative work for my husband's businesses, which were flourishing. For the first time, we weren't living paycheck-to-paycheck, and

---

161 John 6:35
162 Mark 10:29-30

I'd get to stay home and manage the paperwork side of things. It would leave me enough free time to relax and write without the more stressful aspects of running a business with clients and employees. Paperwork? Easy-peasy.

Only, it wasn't. I almost immediately discovered an oversight in something we should have been doing for years. I call it the Great Paperwork Debacle of 2019, and it was a bureaucratic nightmare. It was the only thing I worked on for almost a year, and I'm not caught up on it yet. Writing and art got shunted to the back burner. Actually, art got shoved out of the kitchen altogether. And ease? Well, I felt like God had handed me that gift only to yank it back at the last second.

The point is the Great Paperwork Debacle produced a crisis of faith in me, because deep down, I wanted ease more than I wanted God. I wanted my life to be comfortable more than I wanted Him.

I couldn't have told you this; I didn't even realize it for a long time. When I think of it now, I'm baffled. "*This* was my crisis of faith? What a spoiled, first-world brat I am!"

But there you have it: I didn't really believe that He would give me something better than "easy."

But guess what? Once I finished my toddler-style temper tantrum (which lasted several months), surrendered, and started seeking Him, He did.

The writing of this book has been a balm to my soul. I was weary from seeking water in dry streams—from seeking the good life now with a little Jesus on top instead of the best life forever and making Jesus everything.

I wasn't treating Him like bread; I was treating Him like icing—what's the point if you don't also get the cake, i.e. a comfortable life on this earth?

And in using that analogy, I just revealed something else about me—dare I say—about us.

We want cake. We don't want necessities; we want indulgence. We don't want nourishment; we want a treat. We don't want dinner; we want dessert.

We try to live off the fulfillment of our wants and desires instead of our needs. We feed our souls the cake of entertainment and excess and comfort, yet are somehow surprised when they become fat and lethargic and unable to finish the race.

The things of this world are nothing but empty calories, bloating our lives and running us down instead of providing the life-giving nutrients we need.

In *A Hunger for God*, John Piper says, "If you don't feel strong desires for the manifestation of the glory of God, it is not because you have drunk deeply and are satisfied. It is because you have nibbled so long at the table of the world. Your soul is stuffed with small things, and there is no room for the great."

Jesus was not being hard on the young man when He told him to sell all his things; He was telling him to make room for the great things of God, but the man could not.

He'd already become accustomed to depending on it. If I had already been living the easy life, I wonder how much more it would have taken to wrest it from my grasp?

That is why after this conversation, Jesus told His disciples, "It is easier for a camel to go through the eye of a needle than for a rich person to enter the Kingdom of God."[163] It's too easy for

---

163 Mark 10:25

the rich man to believe he has all he needs and to put his hope in this world.

Paul reminds us of this in I Timothy 6:17: "As for the rich in this present age, charge them not to be haughty, nor to set their hopes on the uncertainty of riches, but on God, who richly provides us with everything to enjoy."

Jesus wants us to be satisfied in Him, because He's the only thing that satisfies.

I eventually handed up worldly ease, and in its place, God is teaching me how to live in His rest *with* the burden He's given me—the one that's light and easy[164] no matter the circumstance.

What kingdom is God trying to wrest from your hand? Do you trust that He will give you something better in its place?

James 1:16-17 says, "Do not be deceived, my beloved brothers. Every good gift and every perfect gift is from above, coming down from the Father of lights, with whom there is no variation or shadow due to change."

Don't be afraid of what you'll get from Him. He's a good Father, and if you pray for bread, He won't give you a stone.[165] He will give you the Bread of Life—and as the passage mentioned earlier says, "a hundredfold" of whatever you place in His hands without reservation. I don't know exactly what that looks like. If you give up the hope of having children, maybe He will show you the tiny, miraculous newborns or the gangly, pimply teenagers at your church and say, "These are your children." If you give up your dream career, maybe an opportunity you thought was out of your reach will show up on your doorstep.

C.G. Trumbull says in *Messages for the Morning Watch: Devotional Studies in Genesis:* "That is just the way God meets every real sacrifice of every child of His. We surrender all and accept

---

164 Matthew 11:30
165 Matthew 7:9

poverty, and He sends wealth. We renounce a rich field of service; He sends us a richer one than we had dared to dream of. We give up all our cherished hopes, and die unto self; He sends us the life more abundant and tingling joy. And the crown of it all is our Jesus Christ."

Like Abraham taking Isaac up the mountain to surrender him, we find our sacrifice returned to us, fulfilling the promise we thought we had relinquished forever. Sacrifice is a phoenix, burned up in fire, and borne anew from the ashes, just like Christ Himself.

But I don't want to ignore the bit about getting that hundredfold "with persecutions." It feels sort of like God snuck it in—"Oh, yeah, and that hundredfold comes with a side of persecution, but eventually, you know, eternal life." But it simply continues what we see in Christ's sacrifice as well as the refrain of all Scripture—in this life, we will have trials,[166] and the sacrifice may very well be painful.

God wants us to know, as we discussed in the chapter on suffering, that on this side of heaven, all the good He gives will not exempt us from the troubles of this world. But He has overcome the world[167]—not by preventing troubles but by transcending them. Just as death has lost its sting[168] though we must still pass through it, this world's troubles no longer have any power over us. The peace comes alongside the burden to fill us with joy. We can rejoice *in* troubles instead of having to wait until we're trouble-free to rejoice. We are more than conquerors despite tribulation, or distress, or persecution, or famine, or nakedness, or danger, or sword.[169]

166   John 16:33
167   John 16:33
168   I Corinthians 15:55
169   Romans 8:35-37

That is overcoming. And that overcoming means we can release anything God asks without fear.

The devil told me that ease would satisfy. He told the rich young ruler that money would satisfy. Maybe he is telling you it's marriage or accolades or building that house you always wanted or something as simple as getting that new shirt.

It's a lie. No matter how good any of those things might be, they will never fill the dark pit in your soul, but "Blessed are those who hunger and thirst for righteousness, for they shall be satisfied."[170]

In an address after his ninetieth birthday, George Mueller said the following: "I was converted in November, 1825, but I only came into the full surrender of the heart four years later in July, 1829. The love of money was gone, the love of place was gone, the love of position was gone, the love of worldly pleasures and engagements was gone. God, God alone became my portion. I found my all in Him; I wanted nothing else. And by the grace of God this has remained, and has made me a happy man, an exceedingly happy man, and it led me to care only about the things of God."

Jesus isn't trying to take satisfying things away from you; He's trying to give you the supreme satisfaction.

But you have to let Him. You have to *believe* Him.

Let go of the world, and hold on to Him with both hands. He will not disappoint.

---

170 Matthew 5:6

TAKEAWAYS:
- It's not wrong to want good things on this earth unless seeking them gets in the way of seeking God.
- The more things that tie you to this world, the more difficult it is to prioritize Heaven.
- God isn't just an intellectual exercise. Belief is something you do, not only something you think.
- Jesus isn't something you use to add a nice flavor to your life. He is your sustenance—the Bread of Life.
- If Jesus asks you to give something up, whatever He puts in its place will be a hundred times better!
- Don't try to live off indulgences and excess; the soul needs real nourishment just like the body.
- Jesus wants us to be satisfied in Him, because He's the only thing that satisfies.
- Sacrificing something at His bidding is not the death it feels like it is.

WORRY

Worry does not empty tomorrow of its sorrow. It empties today of its strength.

Corrie Ten Boom

Irony of ironies, as I began this chapter, I was—you guessed it—worried. God keeps doing that...as if He actually wants to *teach* me things, not just have me write about them!

Two days ago, I injured my finger, and it may require surgery. It impedes not only my typing speed but every aspect of life, and this will only get worse if surgery is required. It happened just after I'd committed to several art commissions, but surgery may make my time frame unachievable, meaning I'd have to put off either this book or the art.

Preoccupied and unable to concentrate, I literally wasted an entire day attempting to devise a plan for this, though I couldn't know the outcome until after my doctor's appointment, which was two days away, and even if I had, that wouldn't have changed what I *should* have been doing in the meantime—writing.

I allowed my thoughts to take me captive rather than the other way around.[171] If I believe God can do the impossible[172] (as He

---

171 2 Corinthians 10:5
172 Luke 1:37

says He can), and that He will work things to the good of those who love Him regardless of what happens[173] (as He says He will), then why worry? God's got the situation *either way!*

I was acting as if these promises were simply platitudes and didn't have any meaning in the real world that corresponded to how I live my life. The fact that I was writing on worry forced me to a crisis quickly. I had to resolve my own worries or write the chapter as a hypocrite. Not that I've perfectly accomplished overcoming any of the obstacles I've written about, but I didn't want to actively wallow in worry while imploring you not to.

So, I asked myself, "Do I trust Him or not?" My answer was an emphatic, "Yes!" And that required turning it over to the Lord and giving up my fussing. After all, who is better able to carry it? The almighty Creator of the universe or little old me? (That's rhetorical.)

I know trusting God is easier said than done. Even the disciples weren't great at it when danger and difficulty threatened. Jesus was asleep on the boat when the storm came and the waves began filling it with water. The disciples finally woke Him, and their first question was, "Teacher, do you not care that we are perishing?"[174]

Isn't that how we all respond when troubles hit us and it seems like God's not stirring? "God, where are you? Do you even care?"

We want Him awake and active! He doesn't rush to our rescue at the height of trouble, so we think He's letting us down. But He knows all about the wind and the waves, and He knows just when He's needed.

The command to "fret not"[175] is intended for just these times. We're told to fret not, *even when there's something worth fretting*

---

173 Romans 8:28
174 Mark 4:38
175 Psalm 37:8

over. There would be no need for faith if there were no storms and no need for the "peace that passes all understanding"[176] if circumstances weren't uncertain.

If we can only trust Him when the waves are still and the sailing fine, *it isn't really trust.*

And if I couldn't trust Him with a *potential* finger surgery (much less a definite one), how could I say I trust Him at all?

That would be like if the disciples were still on shore, looking out across the water and noticed some clouds just as Jesus proposed crossing. "I don't know, Jesus. It might storm."

Our response should be, "OK, Jesus, if you say we should cross, it doesn't matter if there are storms or not. Let's go!"

If the journey is God's idea, *He will get you there!*

If we doubt God while we're still standing on the shore, how will we ever learn to trust Him once the waves buffet, the water starts pouring into the boat, and all seems lost? We must learn to relinquish worry there first, or we will never endure trials when they come.

Let's look at another shipwrecked apostle. In Acts 27, Paul was a prisoner en route to appear before Caesar. His ship was tossed off course and blown by the storm for days. It seemed there was no hope of survival, but an angel appeared to Paul and told him everyone on the boat would live. He provided this encouragement to the guards and fellow prisoners: "So, take heart, men, for I have faith in God that it will be exactly as I have been told."[177]

Paul was not panicked and worried. In the middle of the crisis, he was still confident, because he knew God keeps His word.

176 Philippians 4:7
177 Acts 27:25

What did he have that the disciples did not? Let's go back to them and see. Jesus calmed the storm, but still rebuked them. "Why are you so afraid?" He asked. "Have you still no faith?"[178]

And the problem appeared in their response: "Who then is this, that even the wind and the sea obey Him?"[179]

They didn't understand the enormity of *who was in the boat with them*. And neither do we if we think our storms are too big for Him or that He doesn't care.

Paul grasped the mystery of Christ[180] and that He was "able to do far more abundantly than all that we ask or think, according to the power at work within us."[181] He knew there was no storm great enough to overcome the Lord's plans.

The disciples surely had a suspicion that Jesus was the Messiah, but no one was going all out and calling Him that. *Who then is this...?* they asked. They didn't get it.

But *we should*. This is the almighty Creator of the universe who parts the seas and separates the day from night, who commands the wind and waves, who set the sun and stars in motion. Is anything too hard for the Lord?[182]

In *Hudson Taylor's Spiritual Secret* by Howard and Geraldine Taylor, there is a story about Hudson Taylor's reaction when fellow missionary George Nichol brought him news of dangerous rioting at some of the other mission houses. This is what happened after he delivered the message:

"Thinking that Mr. Taylor might wish to be alone, the younger man was about to withdraw when, to his surprise, someone began to whistle. It was the soft refrain of the...well-loved hymn: *Jesus I am resting, resting, in the joy of what Thou art....*

---

178 Mark 4:40
179 Mark 4:41
180 Ephesians 3:4
181 Ephesians 3:20
182 Genesis 18:14

Turning back, Mr. Nichol could not help exclaiming, 'How can you whistle, when our friends are in so much danger?'

'Would you have me anxious and troubled?' was the quiet reply. 'That would not help them, and would certainly incapacitate me for my work. I have just to roll the burden on the Lord.'"

If we know who God is and understand His real power, this is how we should face every trial—not with flippant disregard, but with sober confidence and a dedication to the duty the Lord's given us today. Notice the song Taylor whistled. If you don't know the lyrics, look them up. It wasn't a carefree tune as if all was right with the world. It was a song to remind him of the unfailing promises of the Lord, of His steadfast love, and of the hope of eternity.

We should all have a go-to verse or song that brings to mind the unchanging love of God and His purpose in our lives to bring us closer to Him in the midst of whatever dark trial is before us.

Wherever you are, the Lord is in your boat. Whether your financial security is threatened by a market crash, your child seems lost to addiction, or you're broken from the pain and violence you see all around you, He has said He "will never leave you nor forsake you."[183]

Jeremiah 7:7-8 says, "Blessed is the man who trusts in the Lord, whose trust is the Lord. He is like a tree planted by water, that sends out its roots by the stream, and does not fear when heat comes, for its leaves remain green, and is not anxious in the year of drought, for it does not cease to bear fruit."

J. Hudson Taylor and Paul have both just given us glimpses of what that man looks like. I want to be that person, unfazed by storm and drought and danger because I am rooted in the Lord.

---

183 Hebrews 13:5

Jesus says, "Do not be anxious about your life, what you will eat or what you will drink, nor about your body, what you will put on. Is not life more than food, and the body more than clothing?"[184]

If we're not to worry about our most basic human needs of survival, surely, we should not worry about anything else! Yet, if we're honest, most of us will say we spend many hours worrying about where our provision will come from—basic and beyond.

Worry is the most socially acceptable sin there is. We don't think of it as a sin, but at its root, it's a fundamental lack of belief in God's promises. It denies His power and His word. "Fret not" and "do not be anxious" are given in the imperative. They are not suggestions; they are commands.

But as with most of the "have-tos" in the Bible, it's more about "get to." It's freeing us, not enslaving us. Because of Jesus, we can relinquish that load of worry, and as Taylor said, "roll the burden on the Lord." Why would we choose to continue carrying it?

And yet we do. Like a toddler with a security blanket, we cling to it just as the disciples relied on the boat and their own feeble attempts to bail out the water instead of Jesus. They had God in the boat and didn't even think to ask Him for help!

"Many are the plans in the mind of a man, but it is the purpose of the Lord that will stand."[185]

Instead of turning our worries over to Jesus, we turn to earthly resources and our abilities and people, piling burden on top of anxiety—neither biblical. The Lord knows every earthly thing we cling to can be snatched away from us in a moment.

---

184 Matthew 6:25
185 Proverbs 19:21

He wants to be our security. "How often would I have gathered your children together as a hen gathers her brood under her wings, and you were not willing!"[186]

All our fussing and planning cannot stave off trouble, for "which of you by being anxious can add a single hour to his span of life?"[187]

"Therefore, do not be anxious about tomorrow, for tomorrow will be anxious for itself. Sufficient for the day is its own trouble."[188]

Worry is like packing our luggage with everything we might ever need for every journey—even ones we may never take—then trying to carry it all with us everywhere we go. It's impossible and useless and silly.[189]

The next time it rears its ugly head and you're tempted to engage those anxious thoughts, remind yourself of God's promises and His identity. And remember that He's in your boat.

TAKEAWAYS:
- Worry is a waste of time and energy.
- Worry takes your focus off God and His work.
- If we engage in worry, then we don't *practically* believe in God's power, sovereignty, promises, or love.
- Faith is the opposite of worry. You can't actively participate in both; you must choose one or the other.

186 Matthew 23:37
187 Matthew 6:27
188 Matthew 6:34
189 (I'm nearly certain I stole this idea from someone, but I can't remember who. It's similar to an idea in the preface of *The Great Divorce* by C.S. Lewis, though he isn't talking about worry, and similar to two different Corrie Ten Boom stories, though it's not either. Forgive me for any lack of attribution to the rightful smarter-than-me person who first spoke it.)

- Worry is often a lack of trust before trouble even strikes. If you can't trust Him with imaginary fears, how will you ever trust Him with real ones?
- If God doesn't want us to worry about food and clothing—the most essential of all essentials—He most certainly doesn't want us to worry about anything else!
- Worry is nothing but a security blanket giving us a false sense of control.
- Remember who God is and that He's in your boat!

DREAMS

Let not our longings slay the appetite of our living.

Jim Elliot

Pursue your dreams.
Follow your heart.
Aim for the stars.

Yes, I'm talking about those dreams—the ones society touts as a cure for your humdrum, work-a-day life—the ones that are all tangled up with your identity and your passion and your purpose.

I used to have one. I wanted to be a Christian singer/songwriter. I felt a desperation for it like nothing else. I thought if I couldn't do it, I wouldn't be fulfilling my purpose—wouldn't be able to serve God the way He meant for me to, and if I came to the end of my life without achieving it, I would be a failure.

Progress toward its realization left me elated; setbacks left me depressed. It was all-consuming.

To put it plainly, the dream became my god, and it wasn't a good god. It was fickle and petty. It had me living in fear, convinced I was worthless without it and that I'd never be good enough.

Pursuing a career in music was not creating a whole, healthy, faith-filled Christian, but a doubtful, sick, anxious one. My dream had become a corruption rather than a worship. It wasn't even bearing good fruit within me; how could I have expected it to do so for others? For "every healthy tree bears good fruit, but the diseased tree bears bad fruit. A healthy tree cannot bear bad fruit, nor can a diseased tree bear good fruit."[190]

My intentions were good; I really did want to serve God with a gift He gave me, but my poor understanding of what serving God meant left me tied up in knots and spinning around in a sort of whirlpool of defeat. I had made it about me and my gifts and desires rather than about God and His power, and it had left me fearful and desolate.

I was in real danger of becoming the type of artist C.S. Lewis warns about in *The Great Divorce:* "Every poet and musician and artist, but for Grace, is drawn away from love of the thing he tells, to love of the telling till, down in Deep Hell, they cannot be interested in God at all but only what they say about Him."[191]

But for grace, indeed. I can't pinpoint one thing that delivered me from this danger, but sometime in my late 20s, I realized anything that left me in that condition wasn't of God. I'm pretty sure it was a long, slow erosion of my confused beliefs about identity and what it takes to serve God—years of truths washing away the jutting edges of my ambition, desire, and push for self-fulfillment.

Whether your dream is a career, an academic achievement, or a deep desire for marriage and children, hear me when I say there is no external circumstance that can inhibit the complete and total fulfillment and purpose of your life in Christ if you trust

---

190 Matthew 7:17-18
191 *The Great Divorce* by C.S. Lewis © Copyright C.S. Lewis Pte Ltd 1946. Extract reprinted by permission.

Him. I'm not saying your dream will be realized; I'm saying that fulfillment is not contingent upon it.

You could work a menial job your entire life, never reach your earthly potential, have your talent overlooked and undervalued, and never marry, yet still bear immeasurable fruit for the Kingdom of God, because your life in Christ is *not dependent upon external circumstance*...unless you let it be.

Like I did. Like so many people I see in our self-centered, find-myself, fulfill-your-purpose culture.

Don't get me wrong; fulfilling your purpose is an amazing thing, and I wish it for all of you. But in the words of that beloved sage Inigo Montoya, "I do not think that means what you think it means."

Or at least, it doesn't mean what *I* thought it meant, and I wasted years chasing a dream when I could've been chasing Christ.

And do you know what you get when you chase Christ?

Fulfillment.

Purpose.

You even find yourself. Your *truest* self. This quote from C.S. Lewis's *Mere Christianity* is so long, but I just can't help it, because he says it so much better than I can.

"Your real, new self (which is Christ's and also yours, and yours just because it is His) will not come as long as you are looking for it. It will come when you are looking for Him. Does that sound strange? The same principle holds, you know, for more everyday matters. Even in social life, you will never make a good impression on other people until you stop thinking about what sort of impression you are making. Even in literature and art, no man who bothers about originality will ever be original whereas if you simply try to tell the truth (without caring two-pence how often it has been told before) you will, nine times out of ten, become original without ever having noticed it. The principle runs through all life from top to bottom, give up yourself, and you will find your real self. Lose your life, and you will save it. Submit to death—death of your ambitions and favourite wishes every day and death of your whole body in the end—submit with every fibre of your being, and you will find eternal life. Keep back nothing. Nothing that you have not given away will be really yours. Nothing in you that has not died will ever be raised from the dead. Look for yourself, and you will find in the long run only hatred, loneliness, despair, rage, ruin, and decay. But look for Christ and you will find Him, and with Him everything else thrown in."[192]

This was, of course, Lewis's way of expounding upon "seek first the Kingdom of God and His righteousness, and all these things will be added to you."[193]

We seem to think our desires and talents reveal our purpose in God's Kingdom, but this is just silly. Quite often, our desires and talents are in God's way, because we're placing our faith in them instead of His plans. The Bible says quite clearly that He will use all who surrender to Him, and that our *weaknesses* will be used to great purpose. I'm not saying He *can't* use our desires or talents. This would also be silly. But to think that your passion or desire or ability is the only thing you're good for in the body of Christ is to disregard large portions of Scripture.

"For ye see your calling, brethren, how that not many wise men after the flesh, not many mighty, not many noble, are called: but God hath chosen the foolish things of the world to confound the wise; and God hath chosen the weak things of the world to confound the things which are mighty; and base things of the world, and things which are despised, hath God chosen,

---

[192] *Mere Christianity* by C.S. Lewis © Copyright C.S. Lewis Pte Ltd 1942, 1943, 1944, 1952. Extract reprinted by permission.
[193] Matthew 6:33

yea, and things which are not, to bring to nought things that are: that no flesh should glory in his presence."[194]

So if you've been reading this chapter thinking you don't have a dream or a calling and feeling left out, take heart. God doesn't need any inherent gifts to bear fruit for the Kingdom. He will use your willingness, your humility, and your love to great purpose wherever you are.

It's the very things we are completely incapable of doing by natural means that bring God the most glory. If someone has all the necessary talent, knowledge, and ability, it's all too easy for that individual to be elevated and God to be left out of it altogether, both in his own mind and the minds of those around him.

Paul says of his earthly qualifications, "…I myself have reason for confidence in the flesh also. If anyone else thinks he has reason for confidence in the flesh, I have more: circumcised on the eighth day, of the people of Israel, of the tribe of Benjamin, a Hebrew of Hebrews; as to the law, a Pharisee; as to zeal, a persecutor of the church; as to righteousness under the law, blameless. But whatever gain I had, I counted as loss for the sake of Christ. Indeed, I count everything as loss because of the surpassing worth of knowing Christ Jesus my Lord. For His sake I have suffered the loss of all things and count them as rubbish, in order that I may gain Christ."[195]

All of Paul's stellar credentials and passion, of which he'd been very proud, meant absolutely nothing once he came to Christ. He had been an up-and-coming star, and he threw his whole ambition out the window and counted it as rubbish.

If you're not willing to give your dream up for God—*even if you want to serve Him with it*—then you are prioritizing it over Him, and it will not end well. Maybe you'll fail and end up ragged

[194] I Corinthians 1:26-29
[195] Philippians 3:4-8

and bitter, unhappy and—very likely—alone. Or worse, you will pursue your goal without waiting for God's counsel, and He will give you your request, but send leanness into your soul.[196]

George MacDonald said, "In whatever man does without God, he must fail miserably, or succeed more miserably."

Success of a dream gained without God's blessing is a joyless place indeed and a hard lesson for those who have pursued it relentlessly only to find the same emptiness in the pit of their souls.

Recognize that if the thought of your unfulfilled dream leaves you desolate, dissatisfied, and desperate, you're likely chasing the dream and the success of the dream rather than the person of Jesus Christ.

I have also seen people use their dreams as an excuse for selfishness and disregarding their responsibilities—families left behind (both literally and figuratively), work neglected, bills unheeded, friends used, commitments forgotten. The dream took precedence over everything.

Friends, if your dream is more important to you than the people you should be loving and serving, it is self-focused, not God-focused.

The first three verses of I Corinthians 13, the "Love Chapter," say it best: "If I speak in the tongues of men and of angels, but have not love, I am a noisy gong or a clanging cymbal. And if I have prophetic powers, and understand all mysteries and all knowledge, and if I have all faith, so as to remove mountains, but have not love, I am nothing. If I give away all I have, and if I deliver up my body to be burned, but have not love, I gain nothing."

If I had become a Christian musician and had the most moving lyrics and the most compelling melodies, if I wrote a book with the most persuasive explanations or the most fantastical

---

[196] Psalm 106:15 KJV

worlds, if I created a piece of art that thousands praised, but I *had not love*…I would be doing nothing more purpose-filled than banging on a kitchen pot or scribbling unintelligibly with a crayon.

Whatever your dream, if its pursuit is hurting you or your family or friends, take a step back. Sometimes even if the dream is of God, we get ahead of Him and start putting it first.

Is its pursuit or lack causing you to be anxious or depressed?

Do you disregard God's principles in order to pursue it?

Is it causing you to consistently miss meaningful moments with your children?

Is it taking a toll on your performance at work?

Does it leech funds you or your family really need for necessities?

Is it keeping you from spending quality time with your spouse?

Do you forgo your private time with God if something to do with your dream interrupts?

Do you back out of your volunteer time in favor of the dream?

This isn't an exhaustive questionnaire, but it's a start. Take time to test the fruit.

I am not trying to be a killjoy. I definitely don't think God makes everyone put their dreams in a box forever lest they become idols. Sometimes, His plan for us involves the unexpected flourishing of something we feared He wanted us to set aside. Sometimes, He asks us to surrender it for a time while we learn how to abide in Him, then He gives it back with wings. And sometimes, as with me and my music, He asks you to put it in His hands, and curiously, you find relief. The dream was a burden, and He removed it. I found I didn't want it at all anymore. Ten years passed before I had even the slightest inclination to pull out my keyboard and write a new song. But when I did, that new song was free of all selfish conceit and ambition and not-enoughness. I could once again see music with childlike delight—something miraculous like fireflies and thunderstorms and the smell of the ocean.

Try to look at your dream and its pursuit objectively. Hold it in your hands and check it out from all sides. Make sure it's bearing good fruit for you and those around you.

And if you're struggling with knowing your purpose, let me tell you what the Bible says it is:

"He has told you, O man, what is good; and what does the Lord require of you but to do justice, to love kindness, and to walk humbly with your God?" – Micah 6:8

"You shall love the Lord your God with all your heart and with all your soul and with all your mind. This is the great and first commandment. And a second is like it: You shall love your neighbor as yourself." – Matthew 22:37-39

The reduced version of what God finally got through my thick skull back when I was struggling with my dream is this: God cares more about who you are than about what you do. Or in the words of Oswald Chambers, "The only thing that exceeds right-*doing* is right-*being*."[197] Perhaps it would be more accurate to say God cares who you are *before* He cares what you do. He will give you a work and a purpose, but He wants it to be second to your pursuit of Him and your abiding in Him, and it may not be the purpose you thought He had for you.

He wants you to be totally surrendered to His will and loving those around you—faithful in the small things.

A dream clasped tightly for its own sake becomes a little devil—a demanding, exacting thing that never lets up, never gives

---

[197] Taken from *My Utmost for His Highest* by Oswald Chambers, © 1935 by Dodd Mead & Co., renewed © 1963 by the Oswald Chambers Publications Assn., Ltd. Used by permission of Our Daily Bread Publishing, Grand Rapids, MI 49501. All rights reserved.

you a moment's peace, and turns you into a little devil along with it.

A dream placed in God's hands to do with as He will becomes a flower blooming in its season—beautiful, fragrant, and a blessing to everyone who draws near.

TAKEAWAYS:
- If the success or failure of your dream controls your emotions and your sense of self-worth, it has too much power over you.
- Is the pursuit of your dream making you a healthier, stronger Christian or a weaker, more anxious one?
- The fulfillment of your purpose in Christ is not based upon the success or failure of whatever dream you have. Christ's purposes are never dependent upon external circumstances.
- Your purpose and fulfillment will come through God, not through the accomplishment of your dream.
- God gets the glory when He uses us through our weaknesses, not our strengths. He can and does certainly also use talent, ability, and knowledge, but if those seem to be falling by the wayside, *He can still use you.*
- All your dreams are pointless if they don't lead to love and point to Christ.
- If you aren't willing to give up your dream if that's what God asks, then it has become an idol to you.
- Test the fruits; does your dream and its pursuit help or hurt you and those around you?
- Surrendering your dream to God will turn it into the beautiful thing it was meant to be.

CONFORMITY

And his arrangements looked so much like everyone else's that they were unremarkable, though he saw them as something truly distinctive.

Leo Tolstoy, *The Death of Ivan Ilyich*

When I started this chapter, I had no idea how many thoughts about conformity swirled around in my head. That's what writing does. It brings all the random, disconnected thoughts you've ever had about a subject, dumps them in your lap, and makes you sort through them. Some of them are pieces of what you're working on, and some aren't. I've been sorting conformity for a few days now, and I still feel like someone shoved the parts for three different pieces of IKEA furniture at me then burned the instructions.

I can't seem to get going on the right track, so let's just start with what the Bible says: "Do not be conformed to this world, but be transformed by the renewal of your mind, that by testing you may discern what is the will of God, what is good and acceptable and perfect."[198]

Honestly, I could stop right there! I love how succinct that verse is. It not only tells us not to conform; it tells us why.

[198] Romans 12:2

Conformity is making decisions based on worldly wisdom. When we live that way, we don't stop to ask God what He thinks or try to discover His will for us because we think we already have the answers. We try to determine what we should do, what we should have, and what we should think by watching other people. Too often, we simply adhere to the plan that reason dictates, basing our chances for happiness and success on what seems to work for other people rather than looking to God.

This is what the Israelites did when they rejected God as their King in I Samuel 8.[199] They looked around at everybody else. All the other nations had kings—men they could hear and touch and see—men who would make strategies they understood to keep them safe and fight their battles.[200] The Israelites wanted one, too. They were tired of not knowing their next steps. They didn't like all this "trust me" stuff.

Following God feels risky because we never know where He may lead. It requires a relationship with communication and a modicum of worldly uncertainty.

Oswald Chambers says in the April 29th devotion from *My Utmost for His Highest*, "Certainty is the mark of the common-sense life; gracious uncertainty is the mark of the spiritual life. To be certain of God means that we are uncertain in all our ways; we do not know what a day may bring forth. This is generally said with a sigh of sadness; it should rather be an expression of breathless expectation. We are uncertain of the next step, but we are certain of God."[201]

One of my favorite sections from *The Chronicles of Narnia* by C.S. Lewis is in *Prince Caspian* when Aslan appeared only to Lucy.

---

[199] I Samuel 8:7
[200] I Samuel 8:19-20
[201] Taken from *My Utmost for His Highest* by Oswald Chambers, © 1935 by Dodd Mead & Co., renewed © 1963 by the Oswald Chambers Publications Assn., Ltd. Used by permission of Our Daily Bread Publishing, Grand Rapids, MI 49501. All rights reserved.

She knew he meant them to follow, but no one else had seen him, and the way looked steep and precarious. So, they took the safe road, Lucy grieving the whole way. They eventually came upon an enemy outpost, and, of course, had to go back and take the way Aslan had shown Lucy after all. When she met him again, she began to feel guilty for not following and said, "How could I—I couldn't have left the others and come up to you alone, how could I? Don't look at me like that…oh well, I suppose I *could*. Yes, and it wouldn't have been alone, I know, not if I was with you."[202]

The Israelites wanted certainty—the commonsense life—the safe road, by human standards. They wanted a real, flesh-and-blood leader with a solid, earthly plan they could get behind. They didn't understand that earthly plans are anything but solid and that being able to see your next step doesn't always mean it's a good one.

But we'd rather have a clear-cut trail—a one-size-fits-all, cookie-cutter plan that leads, at least, to earthly stability if not success. But if we're honest, we can see that not even the world works that way. I could precisely follow in the footsteps of someone I admire, and there's no guarantee it would take me to the same place.

We can't usually see to the end of God's plans, but we *can* know that they are always good! "'For I know the plans I have for you,' declares the Lord, 'plans to prosper you and not to harm you, plans to give you hope and a future.'"[203]

We can't truly see to the end of our own plans either; they're simply the most rational given our imperfect, incomplete knowledge. They give us only the illusion of control and safety, but God gives us the *promise* of hope and a future! If only we would act like we believe it and live in "breathless expectation," as Chambers

[202] *Prince Caspian* by C.S. Lewis © Copyright C.S. Lewis Pte Ltd 1951. Extract reprinted by permission.
[203] Jeremiah 29:11 NIV

says! God's guidance is always for the good; we can't say that of humans.

Life is like a complex maze with innumerable twists and turns and unfathomable variables and outcomes. Conforming to others' ideas is akin to listening to someone else farther along in the maze because they haven't hit a wall yet. But just because someone's ahead of you in a maze doesn't mean they have taken the right road. They very possibly didn't even start at the same place as you and are likely on a totally different path.

God is the only one standing above the labyrinth, seeing the pattern and knowing the turns we need to take to escape the traps and dead ends. When we have the almighty God and King giving us direction, why would we choose, like the Israelites did, a fellow man, muddling his own way through?

They fell prey to that old "thief of joy"—comparison. And comparison is almost always followed up with either pride and complacency or discontentment and insecurity—none of which have a place in the Christian walk.

Without a king, it was hard for the Israelites to figure out how they measured up. After all, "My king is better than your king" only works if you have a king people can see.

If you are basing your life decisions on standards the world doesn't understand, i.e. being led by God as your King, there's nothing to compare. Your goals will be different, your methods will be different, and your priorities will be different. Keeping up with the Joneses doesn't even make sense when your only direction is Christ.

If we are "imitators of God"[204] as we should be, comparison won't even enter into our lives, because our satisfaction will be in the Lord no matter what our circumstances are. "And the Lord

204 Ephesians 5:1

will guide you continually and satisfy your desire in scorched places and make your bones strong; and you shall be like a watered garden, like a spring of water, whose waters do not fail."[205]

Conforming to worldly ideas will only lead us back to worldly priorities, which are always flawed, narrow, and uninspired. We will begin to idolize all sorts of low, self-centered ideas—nationalism or materialism or legalism or individualism. "Isms" (and kings) are easier to follow than God, because they're straightforward. They have rules and plans we can follow.

But following these things puts us distinctly at risk for leaving God out of the equation altogether. As Oswald Chambers says, "Are you drawing your life from any other source than God Himself? If you are depending upon anything but Him, you will never know when He is gone."[206]

That's what the Pharisees had done with their rigorous legalism. They had created a complex system of dos and don'ts that had none of the grace and love for humanity God intended, but it certainly allowed them to compare themselves to others.

I'd wager we each have a unique combination of isms we conform to.

In America, I think materialism is on nearly everyone's list. We often unseat God as King in favor of decisions that get us nice stuff—or what we think of as the "right" stuff—because that seems like it will bring us contentment. We think having houses and clothes that look at least *close* to as cool as everyone else's will make us happier, when, really, it's just basing our happiness on something fleeting and trivial. For "man looks on the outward appearance, but the Lord looks on the heart."[207] And which do

---

205 Isaiah 58:11
206 Taken from *My Utmost for His Highest* by Oswald Chambers, © 1935 by Dodd Mead & Co., renewed © 1963 by the Oswald Chambers Publications Assn., Ltd. Used by permission of Our Daily Bread Publishing, Grand Rapids, MI 49501. All rights reserved.
207 I Samuel 16:7

you think is more important? It's easy to become slaves to materialism's ever-changing whims just as God warned Israel they would be slave to their kings—taxed and conscripted into service.

And isn't that what materialism does? It takes our funds and puts us in a cycle of consumerism that keeps us working for someone else's benefit simply because we want to conform to society's expectations.

In Galatians 1, Paul says, "Do I seek to please men? For if I still pleased men, I would not be a bondservant of Christ."[208]

Until we stop seeking to please men with our conformity, we can't be totally dedicated to Christ.

For the record, I'm not saying having nice things is inherently sinful. You can be a fully dedicated Christian with a beautiful home. I'm talking about a degree of conformity that replaces God as King in your life, makes you covetous, takes your time away from the things of the Lord, and uses up resources God would have you allocate elsewhere.

There is always something we're tempted to put on His throne, and in doing so, we will become slaves to that instead of to Him.

If we ever manage to put God and God alone in that place, we will finally be free from the rigorous rollercoaster of people-pleasing. No matter your "ism," it will always be a fickle, ever-changing king that will not let you rest in your efforts to measure up.

If we follow God, even when those around us say we're being foolish and going the wrong way, we will never be alone, because He will be with us. Our minds will be *transformed* rather than *conformed*, and we might find that God is calling us to all sorts of things that seem...well, countercultural.

If we're to "walk by faith, and not by sight,"[209] then it stands to reason our faith may sometimes guide us to do things our "sight"

---

208 Galatians 1:10
209 2 Corinthians 5:7

never would. After all, much of what God asked of His followers seems a little eccentric, if not downright foolhardy.

At God's direction...

...Noah built a boat when no one had ever even seen rain.

...Abraham packed up and moved with no idea where he was headed.

...Moses chose to live life as a mistreated outcast rather than enjoying a life as royalty, then went back into the pharaoh's court where he was wanted for murder in order to display impossible feats with the help of his brother and a magic stick.

...Gideon led 300 men against 135,000 at God's command, though there were more troops available.

...Hosea married a prostitute.

...John the Baptist lived in the desert and made his own clothes out of animal skins, living off bugs and wild honey, and insulting the powerful religious leaders while preaching the arrival of this controversial Messiah.

...the disciples all quit their jobs to follow an unknown teacher into an indigent lifestyle.

Can you imagine people making these decisions in modern times? Most would face a lecture about God wanting us to use our common sense.

You can't just pack up your life and start driving with no destination plotted.

At least get a degree as a backup plan.

You can follow Jesus between fishing trips; don't give up your livelihood.

But if these are the kinds of things God asked of His followers in the Bible, why do we seem to think He will only direct us to things that fit our current understanding of what makes a smart, responsible decision?

What makes sense to the world is not always what God would have us do.

We don't like the idea of seeming foolish, but the Bible explicitly says that the world will not understand us and will think us so: "For the word of the cross is folly to those who are perishing, but to us who are being saved it is the power of God."[210] It says, "For the foolishness of God is wiser than human wisdom, and the weakness of God is stronger than human strength."[211] It says we are to trust in the Lord with all our hearts and not lean on our own understanding.[212] We're to be "set apart as holy...."[213]

If this is true, then it follows that God will lead us to do some things that the masses consider foolish, that go against our own understanding, and that set us apart from the world.

It's human nature to want to fit in, but chasing the imperishable rather than the perishable will often have us off the beaten path.[214] We may get some weird looks and shakes of the head from the worldly-wise, but what we gain by not fitting in is the path to true satisfaction, fulfillment, and hope. If we choose to follow the course of conformity, we are choosing—as the Israelites did—a limited, flawed path based on human understanding instead of the almighty, all-knowing, infinitely loving God as our guide.

The Israelites wanted a plan they could understand. So do we. We want our prudent careers and our sensible middle-class houses—preferably upgraded with granite countertops. (I'm stepping on my own toes here, so don't worry if I'm stepping on yours.) We want our kids to go to college, and we want to save up for retirement. And maybe that's what God has for you. But maybe it's not.

210 I Corinthians 1:18
211 I Corinthians 1:25
212 Proverbs 3:5
213 2 Timothy 2:21
214 I Corinthians 9:25

What if sometimes Christian nonconformity looks more like a calling for your family to live in a tiny apartment, clothe your kids in hand-me-downs, drive an old beater, and eat mostly ramen noodles and tuna salad because that is where you can best serve others?

What if it looks like working a janitorial position at a school even if you have a college degree because God knows there's a kid there who needs something you can give?

What if it looks like giving people the benefit of the doubt when they don't deserve it?

What if it looks like turning the other cheek?[215]

What if it looks like losing your job because you wouldn't agree to do something morally ambiguous?

And while I'm on the subject, if we really want to be nonconformist, we should live our lives with joy instead of cynicism, hope rather than doubt, contentment instead of complaint, kindness instead of impatience, and forgiveness rather than blame.

Now, that's some nonconformity I can get behind!

Notice in those examples that the goal is our continued sanctification and doing God's work, not the earthly path to security and a trouble-free life. Unity with Him and abiding in Him is always the goal, because only by abiding in the vine[216] can we bear fruit.

And abiding in the vine sometimes means walking through the valley of the shadow of death where worldly wisdom would tell us never to go, but it also means that God is with us there.[217] It sometimes means there are mountains to climb but also that God will make a way.[218]

215 Matthew 5:39
216 John 15:4
217 Psalm 23:4
218 Isaiah 49:11

The "right" way culture says to do things is not always the way God would have us do them. Culture would often have you chasing nothing more meaningful than creature comforts or the latest fashion, whereas God's way is always full of depth and beauty even if that beauty is mixed with sorrow and trials.

I'm not saying you should choose the road less traveled just because you feel like it. God has different plans for each of us. Maybe some of us with grand ideas need a little mundanity in our lives to check our arrogance, and maybe some of us who live fearfully need to step off the beaten path in order to learn how to trust God.

If you're unwilling to go against social norms when God calls, you will find, at bottom, a lack of trust. Worldly wisdom won't satisfy or sustain you, just as the Israelites' flawed human kings did not provide the security and stability they hoped.

God is ever constant; He is not a man that He should change His mind.[219] Taking His pathway requires an attentive ear and taking one step at a time in His presence, but it is the way of peace and fulfillment. He is a loving Father guiding a child through a tangled labyrinth—this complex world—and our attempts to solve it without Him only serve to drive us deeper into its depths.

So, let us speak—and live and work—not to please man, but to please God who tests our hearts.[220]

May He find that we truly love Him with all our heart and soul[221] and may we allow nothing else on His throne.

---

219 Numbers 23:19
220 I Thessalonians 2:4
221 Deuteronomy 13:3

TAKEAWAYS:
- Conformity does not require a life of faith; it is simply doing what makes sense based on what we see other people doing.
- What seems to make sense to us is not always the best choice, because we can't see all the variables—but God can.
- Conformity inevitably leads to comparison, which takes us into pride or despair, neither of which are traits Christians should bear.
- What reason dictates will vary wildly depending on when and where you were born, how you were raised, and your personal biases. There is no universal human system you can follow and have any guarantees.
- If you are trying to follow in the self-sacrificial footsteps of Christ, conformity will have you aiming at the wrong goals.

REGRET

Regret feels bad about past sins. Repentance turns away from past sins. Regret looks to our own circumstances. Repentance looks to God.

Kevin DeYoung, *The Hole in Our Holiness: Filling the Gap between Gospel Passion and the Pursuit of Godliness*

On the front end, it's hard to tell the difference between regret and repentance. They both look like grief and remorse and sorrow. But the outcome reveals all.

Regret brings stagnation and paralysis; repentance brings change and forward motion.

People in the grip of regret become defeated shadows; people in the grip of repentance become warriors for Christ.

Regret is self-focused; repentance is God-focused.

We all mess up. We all do things we know are wrong even as we do them. So, how do we move on when we've crossed a line and we know we're guilty?

If there's anyone in the Bible who could've ended up shrouded in regret, it's David. He stole Uriah's wife and had him murdered to cover it up.

I always thought the way Nathan called him out was such a poignant use of story:

"There were two men in a certain city, the one rich and the other poor. The rich man had very many flocks and herds, but the poor man had nothing but one little ewe lamb, which he had bought. And he brought it up, and it grew up with him and with his children. It used to eat of his morsel and drink from his cup and lie in his arms, and it was like a daughter to him. Now there came a traveler to the rich man, and he was unwilling to take one of his own flock or herd to prepare for the guest who had come to him, but he took the poor man's lamb and prepared it for the man who had come to him."[222]

David was outraged by this. "This man must die!"[223] he said.

Then came Nathan's response: "You are the man."[224]

You are the man. Talk about a knife to the heart. Can you feel the shame washing over David as he recognized himself in that story? He had displayed greed, lust, power, and covetousness in a total disregard for anyone but himself. He placed his own desires and reputation above another man's life, and as punishment, God said the child Bathsheba was carrying would die, making David responsible for the death of his own son.

This is the kind of guilt that could send a man spiraling into endless despair.

And David does grieve. Psalm 51 is dense with his sorrow and repentance. "Have mercy on me, O God, according to your steadfast love; according to your abundant mercy blot out my transgressions. Wash me thoroughly from my iniquity, and cleanse me from my sin! For I know my transgressions, and my sin is ever

---

[222] 2 Samuel 12:1-4
[223] 2 Samuel 12:5
[224] 2 Samuel 12:7

before me."[225] "Create in me a clean heart, O God, and renew a right spirit within me."[226]

"My sin is ever before me," David said. He knew he would never forget what he'd done and the terrible consequences, but he wanted renewal; he wanted to be in fellowship with God again.

When David and Bathsheba's son fell ill, he spent seven days fasting and praying in isolation, but once the news came that the child had died, David got up, took a bath, worshipped the Lord, and ate breakfast.

I think some of us would've gotten stuck here. We think that because our sins have consequences, God is still angry; His forgiveness is not yet complete. And if we think He hasn't forgiven us, how can we forgive ourselves?

But even in their initial conversation, when David was on the front end of repentance, Nathan said, "The Lord also has put away your sin…."[227]

There was no probation period before the forgiveness was enacted, but David understood that repentance didn't automatically let him off the hook from the consequences.

I'm certain David continued to grieve his son, but the time for grieving his *sin* had passed. He did not allow his shame nor the consequences of his sin to determine how he lived out the rest of his life, even in the short term. He had repented and was forgiven. It was time to move forward.

But *how* did he move forward? He makes it look easy.

David knew that everything good in him came from God anyway. He approached God in humility, knowing he deserved nothing and had no righteousness in himself. He was grieved, but not shocked, at his own depravity. He wasn't hiding behind the lie

---

225   Psalm 51:1-3
226   Psalm 51:10
227   2 Samuel 12:13

that he had it all together. His failures were simply a confirmation of what he already knew—that "there is none who does good, not even one."[228]

"…for no one living is righteous before You."[229]

The secret is in the humility: "…for God opposes the proud but gives grace to the humble."[230] "For You save a humble people, but the haughty eyes you bring down. For it is You who light my lamp; the Lord my God lightens my darkness."[231] "The sacrifices of God are a broken spirit; a broken and contrite heart, O God, you will not despise."[232]

The Bible tells us over and over again that we are sinners and that as long as we are living in this flesh, we will continue to sin: "For I know that nothing good dwells in me, that is, in my flesh. For I have the desire to do what is right, but not the ability to carry it out. For I do not do the good I want, but the evil I do not want is what I keep on doing."[233]

Prior to his conversion, Paul had persecuted Christians with fervor, played a role in the execution of Stephen, and sought the imprisonment of believers, yet he is still able to say, "…but one thing I do, forgetting those things which are behind and reaching forward to those things which are ahead. I press toward the goal for the prize of the upward call of God in Christ Jesus."[234]

He leaves the past in the past and moves forward into the future God has for him.

If we can't move on from our sins, it reveals our pride—we never really believed we were that bad in the first place. We still thought our merit counted for something.

228   Psalm 14:3
229   Psalm 143:2
230   James 4:6
231   Psalm 18:27-28
232   Psalm 51:17
233   Romans 7:18-19
234   Philippians 3:12-13

I still struggle with guilt and shame when I fail, but not in the same way I used to. There came a time when I realized if my feelings about God changed when I messed up, then my faith was not really in God at all, but in myself.

Author Michael Wells says in his book *Sidetracked in the Wilderness*, "...the depth of our unbelief is truly revealed in how we respond to God when we fail. If we wallow, cut ourselves off from Him, and traffic in self-punishment, we reveal the dark depths of unbelief. For in all our self-punishment, we prove that we sensed that our acceptance rested not in the Son of God but rather in how well we could perform."

Do you believe that Jesus's sacrifice cleanses you?[235] Do you believe that God casts your sins into the depths of the sea?[236] Do you believe that He removes your sins as far from you as the east is from the west[237] and that He remembers them no more?[238]

Then who are you to continue bringing them up, hanging on to them, and refusing to move forward in a walk of faith?

God can use you mightily no matter what you've done. David is still called a "man after God's own heart" in Acts 13, and Paul wrote nearly half of the New Testament. If God can forgive them of murder and adultery and persecution of His church, He can cover your poor life decisions or those terrible things you said to your spouse or that accident that was your fault.

David Powlison said, "Are you too bad to receive grace? How could you be too bad to receive what is for the bad?"

If we think our sins are too bad or we've sinned too much for God to bring us back into His will, we don't fully understand the Gospel: "For I am sure that neither death nor life, nor angels nor

---

235 1 John 1:7
236 Micah 7:19
237 Psalm 103:12
238 Hebrews 8:12

rulers, nor things present nor things to come, nor powers, nor height nor depth, nor anything else in all creation, will be able to separate us from the love of God in Christ Jesus our Lord."[239]

Once we are His children, nothing in all creation can separate us from His love—not even our sins and mistakes and regrets.

Jesus said, "Those who are well have no need of a physician, but those who are sick. I came not to call the righteous, but sinners."[240] He knows all about us and our weakness, for "while we were still sinners, Christ died for us."[241]

None of the ruminating regrets that plague your unsleeping mind at 3:00 a.m. are bad enough to keep you from carrying out the rest of your life in God's will, but Satan loves to keep you mired in them: "For godly grief produces a repentance that leads to salvation without regret, whereas worldly grief produces death."[242]

Repentance bolsters your immunity to temptation, because its end is forgiveness and healing. Regret is more likely to spiral you back into sin—whether a repeat of the first or a new one—because your guilt is not assuaged, and your spirit is crushed under its weight.

The world preaches the mantra, "You are good enough." Even in Christian circles, this idea is embraced and used to encourage.

But that thought is only helpful when you *feel* like you're good enough—when you're doing the right things and making the right choices. When you mess up, the despondency hits again.

I'm actually NOT good enough. Look what I did. I'm a fraud, a jerk, a loser.

[239] Romans 8:38-39
[240] Mark 2:17
[241] Romans 5:8
[242] 2 Corinthians 7:10

"I am good enough" is not actually very comforting, because we're not, and, deep down, we know it.

Do you know what *is* comforting?

"I'm not good enough, but that's OK. I never will be, but that's OK. I will make more mistakes, but Christ has already covered them."

Our righteousness in Christ is not dependent upon us living perfectly. What is salvation for if not because we need it?

The Bible does make it clear that we should do what we can to right our wrongs.

"Therefore, if you are offering your gift at the altar and there remember that your brother or sister has something against you, leave your gift there in front of the altar. First, go and be reconciled to them; then, come and offer your gift."[243]

Upon following Christ, Zacchaeus paid back everyone he had cheated four times the amount he took.[244]

Is there someone you've hurt? If you can make it right, you should. If you can't, the only purposeful thing you can do is trust it to God and let it go.

Maybe you have tried to right a wrong, but the person you hurt wants nothing to do with you. The Bible even gives instruction for this: "If possible, so far as it depends on you, live peaceably with all."[245]

Give it to God, and move on.

Maybe you wronged someone who has since passed away, and you never got the chance to apologize.

Give it to God, and move on.

---

243 Matthew 5:23
244 Luke 19:8
245 Romans 12:18

Maybe you regret a decision you think changed the course of your life for the worse, and, like David, there is nothing you can do to fix your mistake.

Give it to God, and move on.

When God reveals a place you have failed, mourn your sin. Repent and turn away from it. Come to God in humility. Do what you can to make it right. Then abide in God's forgiveness rather than wallowing in the guilt and shame.

Forget what's behind, trust that God has covered you with His righteousness, and move forward into His call.

TAKEAWAYS:
- The outcome of regret is stagnation and self-loathing.
- The outcome of repentance is change and focus on God.
- Humility is essential for you to move on from your mistakes.
- You should not be shocked at your own sinfulness; the Bible makes it clear you cannot be righteous by your own efforts.
- Trust that all the things God says of your failures are true; they are redeemed by Jesus's sacrifice no matter how bad they are.
- No matter your regret, you can move forward in God's will.

THE CARES OF THIS WORLD

Don't let the noise of the world keep you from hearing the voice of the Lord.

Anonymous

Almost all the obstacles we've talked about can be summed up by Jesus's words in the Parable of the Sower[246]—"the cares of this world and the deceitfulness of riches."

Our fleshly woes and wants take us over and leave little room for the things of God.

We have so much freedom in Christ to pursue our hopes and dreams, to enjoy our days and minutes, our loved ones, our work, and all beautiful things. God gave us good things, and every joy gained through seeking Him will have eternal spiritual value.

The catch is that we shouldn't circumvent God to get those good things nor trust them to fulfill us. The desire to gain them should not drive us ahead without His guidance, and the fear of losing them should not hold us back when He tells us to move.

The pursuit of God should come first, and every earthly action should be colored by it.

Did you ever notice that Satan tempted Christ with things God was going to give Him anyway?

[246] Matthew 13:18-23

Satan offered Jesus bread at the end of His fast,[247] and after Satan departed, the angels came and brought Jesus food.[248]

Satan told Jesus to throw Himself from the highest point of the temple because God would rescue Him.[249] Jesus was cast down in sacrifice, and God raised Him from the dead.

Satan offered Jesus power over all nations and kingdoms,[250] but He was already the King of Kings,[251] and is now seated at the right hand of God, reigning forever from Heaven.[252]

Whatever Satan is tempting you with, it is something the Lord wants to provide, but Satan's prizes are all temporary, tainted, and distorted, whereas God's are eternal, pure, and true.

God didn't only give Jesus bread, but made Him the eternal Bread of Life. God didn't protect Jesus from injury in a fall, but healed Him from the ultimate injury of death to live forever. God didn't give Jesus an earthly kingship, but made Him King forevermore.

The Devil sows weeds among the good fruit God offers us, and it's hard for us to tell the difference, so we eat the bitter, temporary fruit of the weeds and grow spiritually malnourished.

God's blessings often take time, and we don't understand where He's taking us. We don't think He's going to come through, so we poke and prod and experiment on our lives, hoping to land upon the secret.

Satan steps in to assure us we can do it our way using earthly means instead of waiting for God's lead, but we're no more capable of creating a complete spiritual man than Frankenstein was of creating a complete physical one, and we end up cobbling

---

247 Matthew 4:3
248 Matthew 4:11
249 Matthew 4:5
250 Matthew 4:8-9
251 I Timothy 6:15
252 Ephesians 1:20

together a sad, incomplete, tragic imitation. We don't have the knowledge or tools to create the real thing—that takes the Creative One Himself.

Eternal souls must be fed eternal food, and that comes from Christ alone.

He is not only the lightning bolt that invigorates, but the battery that fuels. Without Him, we are spiritual corpses—"for you were dead in the trespasses and sins in which you once walked."[253]

If we continue seeking spiritual fulfillment through the means of this world—by following the passions of our flesh and the desires of our bodies and minds[254]—we will continue walking around with a semblance of life, but feeling, deep within, its lack.

We must stay plugged in to the battery of Jesus Christ. Through Him, we will receive the "immeasurable riches of His grace"[255] and be made whole. If we keep plugging and unplugging, we will live in a bewildering sequence of spiritual highs and lows. If we attempt to plug into some other source, we will either be quite run down or receive a terrible shock and possibly wind up spiritually dead.

Just like you won't get the full benefit of a diet if you only stick to it when you feel like it, you won't experience all the promises of God and exhibit the fruits of the Spirit consistently if you only seek the Kingdom in fits and starts.

But what if we persisted in seeking it?

One day, while browsing the internet, the headline of an article caught my eye: *She Wanted to See What Would Happen if She Didn't Give Up.* The article was about a woman's weight-loss journey, but I started thinking about how it corresponds to our spiritual lives as well.

---

253 Ephesians 2:1
254 Ephesians 2:3
255 Ephesians 2:7

When we diet, we often cheat because we start thinking it's not working or that we'd rather have the short-term payoff of a snack rather than the long-term payoff of weight loss.

The same thing happens in pursuit of the Kingdom of God. We can't see the results right away and start to feel it isn't worth it. We want our rewards now instead of later. If I'm honest, my spiritual life is often like that of a yo-yo dieter. I commit for a while, grow tired, discouraged, and impatient, then go back to my old ways, seeking the things of this world because they feel easy and possible by my own strength.

But what if we kept trying to seek the Kingdom of God even when it was difficult? Even when it seemed unattainable or too far off? What if, like that woman on her weight-loss journey, we found out what would happen if we didn't give up?

We don't have to wait to find out! We're told over and over that we can only be satisfied in Christ:

"In Your presence there is fullness of joy; at Your right hand are pleasures forevermore."[256]

"Jesus said to them, 'I am the Bread of Life; whoever comes to Me shall not hunger, and whoever believes in Me shall never thirst.'"[257]

"For He satisfies the longing soul, and the hungry soul He fills with good things."[258]

"The afflicted shall eat and be satisfied; those who seek Him shall praise the Lord! May your hearts live forever!"[259]

The problem is we maintain our belief that earthly things *can* satisfy. We like the idea of Jesus, but don't really believe that He alone will fulfill us—that He is priceless and worth more than

---

[256] Psalm 16:11
[257] John 6:35
[258] Psalm 107:9
[259] Psalm 22:26

everything we could ever get on this earth. We want Jesus *plus*, not Jesus *only*. We're afraid if we weed out the cares and pleasures of this world, our garden will be stripped bare, so we keep them around—insurance just in case Jesus doesn't work.

We continue pursuing worldly comforts and pleasures and accolades and connections in our quest for fulfillment and joy, then blame God when we are not satisfied. Our longings increase, so we drink more deeply of the world and eat more fervently of its fruit only to find our thirst and hunger aroused rather than slaked.

G.K. Chesterton says in *What's Wrong with the World*, "No man demands what he desires; each man demands what he fancies he can get…the whole is an extravagant riot of second bests.…"

As long as we will accept the counterfeit reward, Satan will continue placing it in front of us. If we live in the frantic fear of missing out rather than in the confidence of God's promises, we will accept it. But it's not only second best, it's a warped perversion of the real thing—a slow poison that, in the end, will leave us starving to death.

The taller we allow the weeds to grow, the more obscured the real fruit becomes. We look around and see towering green all around us and wonder how we can be hungry in the middle of such a lush garden, but we did not choose our crops with care.

Soul-food only comes through seeking Christ, not by going around Him. The crux of the whole thing is something everyone who's spent any time in church has heard a thousand times: "Seek first the Kingdom of God and His righteousness, and all these things will be added to you."[260]

That is the only way to satisfy the depths of your soul's desires. Earthly prizes might satisfy for a time, but they cannot last.

[260] Matthew 6:33

Don't let the cares of this world and the deceitfulness of riches choke the life-giving promises God has for you. Don't settle for second best.

TAKEAWAYS:
- Don't allow your troubles or desires to overtake your pursuit of Christ.
- God wants to give you true, eternal fulfillment; the Devil tempts you with the distorted, temporary version.
- Worldly things will fade away; the things of God will follow us into eternity.
- Our eternal souls are sustained by nourishment from the eternal, not from the things of this earth.
- If we would really seek first the Kingdom of God—and keep seeking it—we would finally find that the rest of the promise would come true and "all these things" *would* be added to us.

SECTION TWO
Building Spiritual Health

PREVENTATIVE MEASURES

The reason why many fail in battle is because they wait until the hour of battle. The reason why others succeed is because they have gained their victory on their knees long before the battle came. Anticipate your battles; fight them on your knees before temptation comes, and you will always have victory.

R.A. Torrey

About halfway through writing this book, I realized that covering only the things we struggle with was not a very healthy way to look at our relationship with God—or anything else for that matter—as if it were only a series of problems to solve.

If you've ever heard the term "positive psychology," you will know what I'm talking about. For years, psychology almost exclusively studied the *problems* regarding emotions and mental health. Someone finally asked, "Hey, what if we found out what actually makes people happy and emotionally healthy to begin with?"

In *The Happiness Advantage*—one of my favorite books on this topic—the author Shawn Achor mentions a time he was invited to speak during a "wellness week" at a prestigious school. "They listed the nightly topics as follows: depression, eating disorders, bullying and school violence, illicit drug use, and for the last night, they were waffling between discussing risky sex or happiness. 'That's not a wellness week,' Achor said. 'It's a sickness week.'"

Lest I be accused of writing a book treating spiritual sickness as inevitable and saying nothing about creating a foundation of spiritual health, I am including some proactive actions and attitudes that diminish the power obstacles to faith have over us.

God gives us precepts and recommendations about how to live joyful spiritual lives in peace and faith and rest. But in the same way we often don't take the doctor's advice about diet and exercise until we're already ill, I'm afraid many of us wait till the spiritual cancer is fully entrenched to apply the disciplines.

Neither God nor the doctors give us guidelines because they want to inhibit our happiness or freedom but because they want us healthy and whole.

A healthy-minded individual attentive to their spiritual habits will find it easier to fight off a spiritual illness, just as a healthy human body is more effective at fighting off disease. And spiritual exercise not only increases your chances of staying well, it also generates a more energetic faith and more endurance when things get tough.

We will touch on some healthy spiritual habits in the chapters to come, but I want to mention here that finding a cancer early is usually a great boon to its cure. If we are alert to our spiritual condition and checking in with the Father, He will identify the illness quicker than we ever could—or keep us from becoming ill in the first place.

And on that note, we will go back to the metaphor in the Parable of the Sower[261] where our obstacles to faith are compared to weeds sown amidst the intended spiritually bountiful crop.

261   Matthew 13:18-23

I, admittedly, don't know much about plants, and I'm not very good at tending them. But earlier this year I had what I'm sure will seem, to real gardeners, a very elementary epiphany about the weeds in my flower bed. I always had a sort of defeatist attitude about pulling them.

What's the point? They'll just come back, I thought.

It's not that pulling them didn't make the flower bed look nicer temporarily, but they always reappeared, strong as ever.

Then I saw the answer to a gardening question posted somewhere: "Just be sure you pull it before it goes to seed, or you'll have a whole crop."

A light bulb went off in my head! If I pulled the weeds early enough, I wouldn't give them time to re-seed and spread, and, each year, there would be fewer and fewer popping up in my flower beds!

Suddenly, weeding no longer seemed pointless and frustrating. I understood that it could make a long-term difference.

The same is true of spiritual ailments. Rooting them out can feel like a futile activity until we recognize that the quicker we pull them up, the fewer we'll have to pull next time.

There is a progression to sin just as there is a progression in the growth of a weed: "But each person is tempted when he is lured and enticed by his own desire. Then desire when it has conceived gives birth to sin, and sin when it is fully grown brings forth death."[262]

It starts with a tiny seed of desire leading to a little sprout of temptation, but it only spreads if we allow it to go to seed, i.e. give birth to sin. We can pull it before it comes to that. If we root it out when it's simply desire or even temptation, we've stopped the process. But the longer we let the weed grow, the more likely it

---

[262] James 1:14-15

will spread and take over. It'll be all mixed in with our flowers and will become harder and harder to extricate without wrecking the whole garden, not to mention the time and hard work involved.

So, let's not wait until the weeds take over or the cancer is already rooted. Let's "put on the full armor of God, so that when the day of evil comes, we may be able to stand our ground, and after we have done everything, to stand."[263]

TAKEAWAYS:
- There are proactive actions you can take to encourage spiritual health, so the obstacles to your faith have less power over you when they arise.
- God doesn't give you guidelines to keep you from enjoying life any more than the doctor does; He does it so you can live a happy, healthy spiritual life.
- Abiding by His guidelines will boost your spiritual immunity.
- The quicker you root out a spiritual weed, the easier it will be to keep those weeds from overtaking you. Don't allow sins to come to fruition and spread.

263 Ephesians 6:13

BELIEF

It is one thing to believe in God; it is quite another to believe God.

R.C. Sproul, *Surprised by Suffering*

As someone who fervently believes God's promises, I wrote this book in the hopes of learning how to act like it.

Cicero the Younger said, "If you want to learn, teach," and though I'm not sure I can call what I've done here teaching, my goal was certainly to organize thoughts for my own edification in such a way that they might also help others.

The process certainly changed me. God did not change; my beliefs about God did not even change. But they grew deeper and more solid as I studied the Word, tested its truths, and considered how it should be expressed in my life.

My intellectual assent to these truths was not enough to help me grow; I had to swim in them, interact with them, and put them into action before they started to genuinely impact my life and my attitude.

Just as a car does not benefit from the mere idea of an oil change but only by the execution of one, my life was not benefiting from Christianity in the way it should have because I was not acting on quite a lot of its promises and precepts; I was simply asserting they were true.

We've all heard the verse: "Even the demons believe—and shudder!"[264]

Clearly, there's a vast difference in "believing" to the point of obedient action vs. simply "believing *in*."

I'm slowly learning to enact this type of belief, and many of the obedient actions God led me to take have been subtle, internal attitude shifts—things like accepting inconveniences with peace instead of frustration, being gracious in the face of others' mistakes, and letting go of my own schedule and agenda. These were conscious decisions to practice His precepts and believe His promises, and they have taken me from stressed to rested, from distracted to focused, from dissatisfied to contented.

When tempted to seek fulfillment elsewhere, I now seem to hear the still, small voice[265] of God ask, "Do you believe Me when I say that only I will satisfy?"

When I am anxious over something, I hear Him say, "Do you believe Me when I say I will work all your circumstances for good?"

When I feel inadequate, His assurance prompts, "Do you believe Me when I say My strength is made perfect in your weakness?"

And fortified with the Word, more and more frequently, I am able to answer, "Yes," and rest in Him.

It comes down to believing Him. So, though I hope the words in this book have brought you closer to that point, they will not be enough to keep you there. Just like any book you read, it will fade in your mind. Besides, it's full of *my* revelations, not yours. Some of them probably did not even resonate with you.

264 James 2:19
265 I Kings 19:12

So I'm going to tell you one way to begin to *really* believe God—that is, simply, to know His Word. Because how can you believe Him if you don't know what He says?

The Bible says it outright: "So faith comes from hearing, and hearing through the Word of God."[266]

And it's not the whiz-kid speed-reading that will make God's Word come alive in you. It's the comprehension that comes with contemplation and meditation.

The Bible repeatedly mentions and gives examples of meditating on God's Word.

- "Blessed is the man who…his delight is in the law of the Lord, and on His law he meditates day and night."[267]
- "Make me understand the way of Your precepts, and I will meditate on Your wondrous works."[268]

Having the promises of God at the ready will fend off all sorts of doubts and fears.

Feeling like the whole world is against you?

- "The Lord will fight for you, and you have only to be silent."[269]
- "You shall not fear them, for it is the Lord your God who fights for you."[270]
- "Do not be afraid and do not be dismayed at this great horde, for the battle is not yours but God's."[271]

---

266 Romans 10:17 KJV
267 Psalm 1:1-2
268 Psalm 119:27
269 Exodus 14:14
270 Deuteronomy 3:22
271 2 Chronicles 20:15

Feeling like you don't know what to do?
- "If any of you lacks wisdom, let him ask God, who gives generously to all without reproach, and it will be given him."[272]
- "Whether you turn to the right or to the left, your ears will hear a voice behind you, saying, 'This is the way; walk in it.'"[273]
- "But the Helper, the Holy Spirit, whom the Father will send in My name, He will teach you all things and bring to your remembrance all that I have said to you."[274]

Feeling afraid?
- "Fear not, for I am with you; be not dismayed, for I am your God; I will strengthen you, I will help you, I will uphold you with My righteous right hand."[275]
- "Have I not commanded you? Be strong and courageous. Do not be frightened, and do not be dismayed, for the Lord your God is with you wherever you go."[276]
- "Be strong and courageous. Do not fear or be in dread of them, for it is the Lord your God who goes with you. He will not leave you or forsake you."[277]

What if you had biblical promises at the ready for anxiety, grief, uncertainty, and the plethora of other struggles you face?

It's easy to think of God in generalities, but sometimes you need something specific. You can't read the whole Bible at once to

[272] James 1:5
[273] Isaiah 30:21
[274] John 14:26
[275] Isaiah 41:10
[276] Joshua 1:9
[277] Deuteronomy 13:6

dig out specific spiritual truths when you're struggling, so make it a little more streamlined.

John Piper says he keeps a notepad beside his chair, and when he comes to a promise of God in the Bible, he writes it down for future reference.

I challenge you to start doing this and to carry those promises with you throughout the day. Write them on cards and hang them on your mirror, your car dash, your office wall, your desk calendar. Schedule them as reminders on your phone. If you're a big dork like me, make a spreadsheet and organize them by category. (I haven't done this yet, but I have plans!)

This is a practical way you can take your thoughts captive[278] and learn to apply the Word. We must train ourselves to think on the things that are true, honorable, just, pure, lovely, commendable, excellent, and worthy of praise.[279]

Whatever works best for you, having these promises on hand—and written upon your heart[280]—will also have the effect of repeatedly turning your thoughts to God. When you see the verse, take the opportunity to say a prayer, and then you will also be learning to pray without ceasing.

And remember that these are weapons! When Jesus was tempted in the desert,[281] He used Scripture to fight off the Devil every time. Having the Sword of the Spirit[282] so fixed in your mind makes a much more formidable weapon than some nebulous idea of God's goodness. That's like a sword that hasn't been properly forged; it will shatter at the most inopportune time, and you will find resisting that much more difficult.

278   2 Corinthians 10:5
279   Philippians 4:8
280   Hebrews 10:16
281   Matthew 4:1-11
282   Ephesians 6:17

Actively reading, learning, studying, and meditating on God's teachings and promises will go a long way toward building your faith. And think what would happen if we fully believed!

Belief isn't only so that you can live in the fullness God promises you; it's also a command, and acting in unbelief has consequences.

I want to be blessed and counted righteous like Abraham and Mary:

- "Abraham believed God, and it was counted to him as righteousness."[283]
- "And blessed is she who believed that there would be a fulfillment of what was spoken to her from the Lord."[284]

...not punished and cut off like Zechariah and the Israelites:

- "And behold, you will be silent and unable to speak until the day that these things take place, because you did not believe My words, which will be fulfilled in their time."[285]
- "So, we see that they were unable to enter because of unbelief."[286]

I sort of already covered this in the chapter on doubt, but I want to make it clear that belief is not a feeling, it's a verb—just like love. You may not *feel* like you believe. You may be absolutely terrified, but if you still strive to put your trust in God and take the steps He asks of you, *you are believing*.

[283] Romans 4:3
[284] Luke 1:45
[285] Luke 1:20
[286] Hebrews 3:19

When you begin climbing the mountain of God's promises knowing them to be solid regardless of what you feel, that is faith. The sturdiness of the mountain is not dependent upon your confidence or bravery. As James Smetham put it, "Mont Blanc does not become a phantom or a mist because a climber grows dizzy on its side."

Our faith, and the work that grows out of it, is based on confidence in the character of God—a character that is the same yesterday, today, and forever.[287] His steadfast love endures forever.[288]

What would change in your life if you lived like you trusted Him? I know how mine is changing. I am happier, calmer, slower to anger, freer, and more hopeful. And that's just a start. I'm finally plugging into the battery instead of trying to charge myself.

You *can* trust Him. Start your list of promises and learn to rest on them. "Taste and see that the Lord is good. Blessed is the man who takes refuge in Him."[289]

God's promises are beautiful, abundant, and—best of all—true.

TAKEAWAYS:
- Believing in God vs. living like you believe what God says are two different things.
- In order to *really* believe God, you must know what He says and know His character.
- Keep a list of the promises God makes as you read the Bible. Categorize them if you're an organizer like me. The important bit is to have them, learn them, and apply

---

[287] Hebrews 13:8
[288] Psalm 118
[289] Psalm 34:8

them. They are weapons against temptation and encouragement when your faith is weak!
- Reading, studying, learning, and meditating on God's teachings are necessities for growing your faith.
- Faith is a verb. You don't have to feel fearless in order to act on God's leading.
- God's promises are not based on how brave you are; they are true and solid no matter how feeble and faltering your steps.
- The outpouring of living like you believe God instead of just saying you do will be the fruits of the Spirit—love, joy, peace, patience, kindness, goodness, faithfulness, gentleness, and self-control.

HOPE

Hope means hoping when things are hopeless, or it is no virtue at all. As long as matters are really hopeful, hope is mere flattery or platitude; it is only when everything is hopeless that hope begins to be a strength.

G.K. Chesterton

I wrote a whole chapter on hope, then realized I'd said a lot of words about hope without actually inspiring any. If there's anything a chapter on hope should be, it's hopeful, so I scrapped that one and here we are.

Hope believes in what it cannot see: "Now hope that is seen is not hope. For who hopes for what he sees? But if we hope for what we do not see, we wait for it with patience."[290]

The hope we have as Christians should be an expectant confidence, not nail-biting anxiety or blind wishful thinking that pretends nothing bad will ever happen.

When the Bible tells us to hope, its objects are always eternal: hope in the Lord, in His salvation, in His mercy, in His Word.

Those things are guaranteed to those who seek Him, and they can't be taken away, but the ease of the voyage is never promised.

[290] Romans 8:24-25

We should have the hope of an adventurer—that is to say, the excited anticipation of shores God has promised we will reach.

If the benevolent god of the sea came aboard as captain, guide, and companion, promising a sailor safe passage to paradise, the sailor would not fear his journey no matter how tumultuous it became. He may endure tsunamis that send him off course or sea monsters that damage his ship or pirates that steal and injure, but through it all, he would look to his almighty captain and know the destination was never threatened. There may also be spectacular sunsets and dolphins gamboling in the waves and the camaraderie of his shipmates.

The same is true of life. It is a sea with waves that rise and fall, and a current that pushes where it will. But whether that be into dangers, loss, or beauty, if we have trusted God as our captain, our destination is sure. Our hope is in Him and His promise.

The sailor does not set his course for a certain wave, call it his destination, and try to stay atop it or claim it for his own. It's a sea; you cannot perch nor anchor on a wave in the deep. The current will always carry you on—sometimes quick and sometimes slow, but never will you stay in one place.

You can fear it or embrace it, but it will carry you along all the same. Setting your sites on one era or circumstance in life as if you could stay there always is as foolish as attempting to live atop a wave. The tide will turn, the crest will crash, and you will be pushed along whether you will or no.

You could look back at a wave and mourn its loss or look forward to another hoping it will fulfill your desires, but any sailor would call you a fool to do so. It's the shore of paradise you're aiming for, and it's that shore you've been guaranteed.

As long as we set our hopes of happiness on the fleeting waves dependent upon time and circumstance, our happiness will be fleeting and dependent upon time and circumstance.

Even the best this world offers must end in one way or another:

Our work will be lost to lay-offs or retirement.

Our relationships will end in rifts or death.

Our possessions will be lost to theft or decay.

The good news is you can enjoy those things along the way. You can feel the power of the wave as it swells and the cool spray on your face as it crests and crashes. You might even reach out your hand and touch it as it passes by, but you cannot *hold* it. The moment you cup it in your hands, it loses something of itself; it is no longer a wave with all the strength and beauty it held only moments before. It's still water and it's still wet, but it's not even very useful as that—you can't drink it. The wave was never meant as sustenance. It will always drip through your fingers and leave you rocking in its wake, but with the memory of its beauty unspoiled as long as you allow it to remain what it was meant to be.

And always, paradise before you and your Captain assuring the way, whether you can see the shore or not. Its sparkling beauty will appear on the horizon one day, and all the waves of joy and sorrow will be as naught. As Christians, what we are hoping and believing for will not be realized *in this world*.

But this world is not without comfort. Christ offers confidence that when you hope in and wait for Him in your distress, He will hear you, He will draw you up out of the pit and set your feet on a rock, He will give you a new song,[291] He will restore the years the locust has eaten,[292] He will fulfill His purpose for you,[293]

291 Psalm 40:1-3
292 Joel 2:25
293 Psalm 57:2

and nothing will thwart it.[294] Hope is the surety that every pain and trouble and trial and every bit of growth and learning is serving something greater than what you can see.

Maybe it's helping to encourage those in the ship with you. Maybe it's leading the ship behind that's lost its way or helping the ship ahead that's taking on water.

In this world, we want to feel like we're making every minute count, speeding toward a goal, and living at peak performance, but God rarely works like that. Many of our biblical heroes spent twenty, thirty, forty, or even fifty years seemingly blown off course altogether or simply languishing in still waters. Joseph was in captivity for thirteen years. Moses was a shepherd in the desert for forty years. Noah began building a boat fifty years before its purpose became clear. Even Jesus did not begin His public ministry until He was thirty.

To those ships charting their own path, the Christian life may look pointless and meandering or even foolish, but those captains do not know the way to paradise, and the God of the sea has not promised them safe passage; they're only barreling ahead in the hopes of getting somewhere, and they hardly even know where they want to end up. Making swift progress isn't helpful if you're going the wrong way.

Maybe you've tried holding onto the wave of your own abilities, riches, looks, marriage, comfort, your job, ease, or friendship, and you've found it spilling from your grasp no matter how carefully you close your hands.

The wave is passing, but the adventure never ends. Even once you reach the shore of forever, it is only the beginning.

If our hope is dependent upon what is happening at the moment or whether we can see a way for things to come out right or

---

294 Job 42:2

not, we very much misunderstand hope. Hope is needed for the journey, not the arrival. We don't have to see the shore or enjoy the wave, because we trust the God of the sea.

But how does one become more hopeful? You can't just decide to be so…or can you?

I actually think it's just that easy…and just that hard. It's not a one-time decision. It takes intentionality and determination. It takes conscious choice and constant turning to the Father every time you fear the coming or the loss of a wave.

Find ways to remind yourself where your unshakeable hope lies. Meditate on some of those promises you've started jotting down:

- "For God alone, O my soul, wait in silence, for my hope is from Him. He only is my rock and my salvation, my fortress; I shall not be shaken… if riches increase, set not your heart on them."[295]
- "By awesome deeds, You answer us with righteousness, O God of our salvation, the hope of all the ends of the earth and of the farthest seas; the one who by His strength established the mountains, being girded with might; who stills the roaring of the seas, the roaring of their waves, the tumult of the peoples, so that those who dwell at the ends of the earth are in awe at Your signs. You make the going out of the morning and the evening to shout for joy."[296]
- "As for the rich in this present age, charge them not to be haughty, nor to set their hopes on the uncertainty of riches, but on God, who richly provides us with everything to enjoy."[297]

295 Psalm 62:5-6, 10
296 Psalm 65:5-8
297 I Timothy 6:17

I have the word "hope" scheduled to pop up as a reminder on my phone three times a day. Sometimes when it chimes, I realize I've started living in fear and grasping at waves instead of resting in God's promises and purpose. The reminder often brings me back into peace.

I also have a list of attitude checks I review each morning. One of these is to consider how I will handle difficult things that come up. Sometimes you know the day ahead has something demanding or frightening in it; sometimes you don't. If you know about a specific hard task in your day, you can plan your hopeful reaction in advance. And when burdens and enemies beset you, you'll be that much further along for having placed hope in your pocket when you started the day. As Galadriel gave Frodo the light of Eärendil's star to carry with him, "It will shine still brighter when night is about you. May it be a light to you in dark places, when all other lights go out."[298]

To be clear, I do not say you should muster hope up as a sort of emotion conjured by will. If you rose early to climb a mountain in order to see the sunrise, you would not say it was your climbing that created the sunrise. The climb only positioned you to see it. You knew the sunrise was there, but there were too many things blocking you from the sight of it.

The same is true of choosing hope and preparing yourself for it. You must put yourself in a position to see its object, and its object is God. We know He is glorious; we just need to make the climb to see Him.

Without an object, hope is merely wishful thinking. This choice you make over and over is that you will continue to turn your face to the one unshakeable object of your hope: Christ and His Word and His promises.

298   J.R.R. Tolkien, *The Fellowship of the Ring*

Living with hope in God's guidance is not happenstance. It's not a feeling of optimism that fades when tested. It's a decision made based on an assurance that cannot be shaken—an expectation of good and a knowledge that the character of God is unquestionably trustworthy: "Let us hold fast the confession of our hope without wavering, for He who promised is faithful."[299]

It is impossible for God to lie,[300] and He has given us this hope so that we might hold it fast—a sure and steadfast anchor of the soul.[301]

The ship may drift and sway, but your soul can remain anchored in the character of God who rules not only the sea, but the universe and time itself.

TAKEAWAYS:
- Hope is an expectant anticipation of what God has promised us.
- Our hope should be grounded in the eternal.
- Everything in this world is fleeting, and if we place our hope in it, that hope will be fleeting as well.
- It may seem like God takes a lot of detours, but only He knows where we're going and what it takes to get there.
- When we trust in God, the destination is never in doubt, no matter how difficult the voyage.
- Eternal hope brings us peace, because we no longer have to find our own way into either purpose or paradise.

---

299 Hebrews 10:23
300 Titus 1:2
301 Hebrews 6:18-19

PRAYER

God gives me whatever I want, because I want whatever He gives.

Saint Therese of Lisieux

I struggled with determining how in-depth this chapter should be. I listened to sermons on prayer, read books, blogs, and many Bible verses about prayer. I talked to my friends and family about prayer and tried new approaches in my own prayer life. I wrestled with what it means to pray in faith while yet understanding that God doesn't give a "yes" to every request we place before Him.

Prayer is intricate and beautiful and mysterious, and I have here only the most cursory of discussions. I trust that you won't consider this chapter a comprehensive study on the topic, but will seek out other resources where my writing leaves off.

When I was 18, I struggled with my belief in God. I *wanted* to believe in Him, but I couldn't feel His presence. I had not yet learned that feelings are a poor compass if it's truth you're after.

One night, in true angst-ridden teenage fashion, I climbed up on the roof to watch the stars. I lay there for a long time contemplating my existential crisis, my Edgar-Allan-Poe-saturated mind awash with all that's bleak and melancholy.

Then I saw a shooting star, and that spark of beautiful death awoke the feeling of hope that had been languishing in my soul.

God, I prayed, *if you're there, let me see ten shooting stars tonight.*

Then I decided that ten was unreasonable. Who had ever seen ten shooting stars in a night? I amended my request.

OK, three…three, and I'll believe You're there.

I don't know how much longer I stayed on the roof, but by the time I climbed down the porch railing, I'd seen eleven shooting stars.

Eleven.

More than I'd asked; more than I'd imagined.[302]

I should've come down from that roof with my face glowing like Moses's when he descended Mt. Sinai.[303] But do you know what happened?

I was still depressed, dejected, and uncertain. The next day I heard there had been a meteor shower.

Ahh, all explained, I thought. *I would've seen those stars anyway. Nothing supernatural about it.*

How could I not see the miracle of great love in the fact that the God of the universe timed this celestial event to perfectly coincide with the night a scared, uncertain girl begged Him for reassurance?

William Temple said: "When I pray, coincidences happen, and when I don't pray, they don't."

Was it a coincidence? Yes. Was it an answer to prayer? Yes. Would there have been a meteor shower if I hadn't climbed up on the roof that night? Presumably…but who can say for sure? Perhaps it would have simply been a different night I climbed up on the roof and made my plea.

302 Ephesians 3:20 NIV
303 Exodus 34:29

Some will say, "Well, of course, if you see one shooting star, a meteor shower becomes more likely, and your subconscious knew that, giving an unfair advantage that the prayer would be answered."

I'd say you were right except I had never cared a whit for stars outside of their beauty. I hadn't the slightest understanding of meteor showers or any other knowledge that would've allowed my subconscious to make such a prediction.

A star fell and my soul leapt, for just a moment, at something outside of myself—something great and huge and incomprehensible. But by the time the eleventh star exhaled its last cosmic light, I'd already begun to see it as commonplace. I wasn't seeking God; I was chasing a feeling.

I had felt God's presence in fleeting flares just like this many times in a laugh or a story or a friendship, but it always departed, leaving the stark emptiness even blacker in its void. I wanted it back. I wanted it to last. I thought the feeling was the goal, or maybe I just thought the feeling meant I was on the right track.

But in either case, without the feeling, I was left floundering and certain either I or the object of my faith was failing.

I think many of us have this same issue specifically with prayer. If you're like me, you can't even count the times you've heard people say something like this:

I just don't feel like God is hearing me.
It's like my words are hitting the ceiling.
I pray, but I don't feel His presence.

In Psalm 13, David prayed, "How long, O Lord? Will You forget me forever? How long will You hide Your face from me?"[304] Yet, he ended that prayer with, "But I have trusted in Your stead-

---
304   Psalm 13:1

fast love; my heart shall rejoice in Your salvation. I will sing to the Lord, because He has dealt bountifully with me."[305]

David knew that the efficacy of prayer is not dependent upon feelings. It's based on who God is, what He's already done for us, and what He says He will do.

Prayer feels mystical—like wishes spoken into the ether—so we think it ought to be accompanied with mystical feelings. And sometimes it is. I have felt God's presence alight like a dove, and I've also felt it hit me in the face like a frying pan (mostly when I'm being absurdly stubborn). But a lack of warm fuzzies is not an indicator of whether God hears our prayer or not, and if we go on chasing that feeling, our prayer life will grow cold and stagnant.

Another falsehood that invades our prayer life is the very human feeling that *doing* something would be better. We seem determined to ask God only when we've exhausted every option that logically presents itself. *Then* we take it to Him.

It's all I can do, we say with a sort of hopeless resignation.

All we can do! Yes, "all we can do" is take our requests to the Creator of the universe, our Father who loves us unconditionally, who bids us ask and receive that our joy would be made full[306] and that we may receive mercy and find grace to help in time of need.[307]

"All we can do" is petition the King of Kings, the Lord of Lords who conquered death[308] and laid the foundations of the earth.[309]

How skewed is our confidence in our own abilities that we think it only worth taking to God after we've tried everything else humanly possible!

305 Psalm 13:5-6
306 John 16:24
307 Hebrews 4:16
308 I Corinthians 15:55
309 Job 38:4

Imagine all our wasted efforts in trying to guess the best solution before we go to Him. What if, instead of relying first on all our worldly wisdom, we took the big things AND the small ones to God from the start? I have a feeling if we'd check in with Him on the front end, we'd hit upon the proper course of action a lot faster!

Here's another feeling that inhibits our prayer life: in short, we fear we're doing it wrong.

We spend about three seconds in focused prayer then realize we're thinking about that meeting we have this afternoon. We try to use words that sound properly reverent and end up feeling fake. We suddenly remember that verse about praying without doubt in our hearts,[310] realize we have doubts, and give up.

For this, I actually have practical advice. So many of the things I read and watched about prayer started out by discussing the mind-wandering that anyone who's ever tried to pray has experienced. They generally follow that up with tips for staying on track. That's all well and good, but I think one reason our minds wander is because we're trying to pray for the things we think we're *supposed* to pray for—lofty, spiritual things or the prayer list from church that's full of people you've never met. Those things feel far away and distant. They don't touch our day-to-day lives, so praying for them doesn't feel personal or relevant to *us*.

Praying for deep spiritual things and for your neighbor's cousin who has cancer should be done, of course, but what if you started your prayers by praying for your "daily bread?"[311] And I don't mean only what you will eat. I mean praying for all the Jesus you need to get through the common, down-to-earth happenings of every day—that you will have grace for that meeting that keeps encroaching on your mind, that the fears your child has about his

---

310 Matthew 11:23
311 Matthew 6:11

test will be calmed, that you won't forget to pick up the milk on the way home.

What if your mind is also wandering because God *wants* to hear about the things it's wandering to? What if God is saying, "Yes, yes, but what about YOU?"

It sounds like I'm saying you should be selfish; I'm not. I'm saying put the oxygen mask on yourself before you try to help others, or you'll be no good to anyone.

I've taken to praying through my to-do list before I pray for anything else. I find that once my mind is clear and calmed from this, *then* I can pray for my neighbor's cousin and actually care about him.

Some of the mind-wandering is undoubtedly just fleshly temptation to focus on worldly things instead of your relationship with the Lord, but that is covered heavily in so many other treatises on prayer, I'm going to leave it to the experts.

If you still have trouble focusing after praying for your daily bread, try writing prayer cards. I got this idea from *A Praying Life* by Paul Miller, and I find it much more doable than a list. A list feels endless and unorganized. If you write prayer cards—one for those needing healing, one for unsaved loved ones, one to focus on your spouse, etc.—you can pick two or three a day and cycle through them. It will also give you a visible record of what you've prayed and when it was answered, thereby increasing your faith.

Another idea is to pray through Scripture. Find a Psalm that speaks your heart. Pray through it verse by verse. This has the double blessing of keeping your mind on prayer while embedding Scripture in your heart.

As for lofty language, throw it out the window. God knows everything in your mind. Why try to speak with fancy words unless that's just how you talk? He knows you, and He loves you as you are. He would not have you come with pretense and pride like the Pharisees[312] or with many words like the Gentiles.[313]

God would have you come in humility,[314] and you don't need any special words to do that. Indeed, you don't need words at all, for "the Spirit himself intercedes for us with groanings too deep for words."[315]

As a parent delights in the unintelligible babblings of a toddler, God delights in the very simplest of prayers, but unlike that parent, God actually understands them.

And when doubts arise, do not despair. I know I've already mentioned it more than once, but the statement "I believe, help my unbelief!"[316]—and the fact that Jesus accepted it—has to be one of the most comforting things in the Bible.

Finally, know that all our prayers are not answered in the way we would like. Death, after all, is a part of this fallen world, and all our prayers for healing cannot be answered or there would be immortal men all around us.

Paul prayed that his "thorn in the flesh" would be removed, but it was not.[317] Jesus prayed that the cup would pass from Him, but it did not.[318] Jesus certainly had enough faith, but God's purposes required that He drink the cup of suffering.

God will only give you good gifts,[319] but sometimes, in the moment, we cannot see the good it will bring. 2 Corinthians 12:7 tells us that Paul's thorn was not removed lest he become conceited. Once Paul understood the good it was doing, he accepted it joyfully. Christ also accepted His suffering, knowing the good

312 Luke 18:11-12
313 Matthew 6:7
314 Luke 18:13-14
315 Romans 8:26
316 Matthew 9:24
317 2 Corinthians 12:7-10
318 Matthew 26:39
319 Matthew 7:11

that would come from His torment and death—"Nevertheless, not as I will, but as You will."[320]

Where our appeals would not further the Kingdom of God, they will never be granted, but we can still trust in the person and purpose of God Himself. He is working for the greatest good even when the path is painful. God is our "refuge and strength, a very present help *in* trouble."[321] It doesn't say there won't be trouble, but that He will help us in it.

I should also make it clear that God will not answer selfish prayers: "You ask and do not receive, because you ask wrongly, to spend it on your passions."[322] And we must ask "in His name." [323] This is not a spell we cast to ensure success; it is an attitude of true submission that desires all be done to His glory. I John 3:22 says, "and whatever we ask we receive from Him, because we keep His commandments and do what pleases Him."

I will admit that my prayer life has, historically, been frightfully lacking. Some of that is due to the things we've already discussed, but I also had the vague idea that living in an attitude of prayer meant I did not need to set aside specific prayer times. We are definitely to be in constant fellowship with the Father—to "pray without ceasing"[324]—but it took me some time to learn the importance of having a dedicated prayer time. It's the difference between talking with your spouse throughout the day and having a date night. Both are needed if the marriage is to succeed practically while yet growing in intimacy.

For years, I also had the misguided idea that prayer was superfluous due to God's omnipotence and sovereignty. It's true that God's great purpose—the redemption of all the earth and those

---

320   Matthew 26:39
321   Psalm 46:1
322   James 4:3
323   John 14:13
324   I Thessalonians 5:17

who choose Him—will be realized with or without my prayers, but the Bible also makes it clear that *prayer changes things.*

"The prayer of a righteous person has great power as it is working. Elijah was a man with a nature like ours, and he prayed fervently that it might not rain, and for three years and six months it did not rain on the earth. Then he prayed again, and heaven gave rain, and the earth bore its fruit."[325]

Joshua prayed that the sun would stand still, and "the sun stopped in the midst of heaven and did not hurry to set for about a whole day. There has been no day like it before or since, when the Lord heeded the voice of a man, for the Lord fought for Israel."[326]

James 4:2 says, "You do not have, because you do not ask."

It doesn't say, "Don't bother asking, because God will give you everything He plans to regardless."

The God who ordered the universe allows our prayers to be forces for good in this world. They are not, as many of us fear, useless whispers into the void. He who tells us to come as little children[327] wants to grant our requests as a parent would a child. He wants us to see that His gifts are good, but we can only do that if we know they came from Him. When He grants something we asked, we can clearly see His hand working in our lives.

God wants an interaction that cultivates relationship. He designed it as such.

How many blessings have I left on the table simply because I did not ask?

Martin Luther said, "I have so much to do that I shall spend the first three hours in prayer."

325 James 5:16-18
326 Joshua 10:13-14
327 Matthew 18:3

He's not the only great Christian who has said as much. Oswald Chambers says, "Prayer does not fit us for the greater works; prayer is the greater work."[328]

May we cease to see prayer as our last resort and begin to see it as the strange and fantastic privilege it is—an invitation into the throne room of our Father, the King, who longs to give us good and perfect gifts.[329]

TAKEAWAYS:
- Feelings are not reliable guides and have no bearing as to whether God is hearing your prayers or not.
- Prayer should be your first response, not your last resort after you've tried everything else humanly possible.
- If your mind wanders while you pray, try praying about the things it is wandering *to*—your "daily bread."
- Don't worry about the words you use in your prayers; God wants your humility and your sincerity, not your performance.
- When doubts crop up, don't despair at your lack of faith; turn that over to God in prayer as well!
- Not all your prayers will be answered in the way you like; God's purposes are sometimes fulfilled in circumstances you'd rather escape.
- Prayer actually changes things. It is for the building up of your relationship with God, but the Bible makes it clear that it also makes things happen that otherwise wouldn't. God wants your interaction.

328 Taken from *My Utmost for His Highest* by Oswald Chambers, © 1935 by Dodd Mead & Co., renewed © 1963 by the Oswald Chambers Publications Assn., Ltd. Used by permission of Our Daily Bread Publishing, Grand Rapids, MI 49501. All rights reserved.
329 James 1:17

FASTING

Christian fasting, at its root, is the hunger of a homesickness for God.

John Piper

When I was a young adult, a non-Christian friend had a co-worker who was fasting, and she asked me about it. He didn't go spend his lunchtimes in prayer or Bible-reading, so she didn't understand the point of not eating. Honestly, I didn't understand it either.

I wasn't raised in a Christian tradition where fasting was emphasized, and it's only been the past few years that I really began to "get it." I knew people in the Bible did it when they were sorely in need of God's guidance, and I had done that a few times over the years, but the overarching concept still eluded me.

Now, I see it as a fundamental way to act out what I believe—chiefly, that God's presence and my relationship with Him is more vital than the most basic of all human needs. I desire Him and need Him above all things.

One of my favorite ways to describe fasting as a general discipline is as a *practice*. When you fast, you *practice* aligning your desires, needs, and will with God's eternal kingdom goals.

If your normal daily life is mostly comfortable, it's difficult to learn to rely on God when hardships arise. Fasting is a way to create a habit of turning to Him in need even when your life is not full of obvious, external desperation. Let me state here that I believe our spirits are *always* in desperate need of God whether we *feel* that desperation or not. But sometimes we learn best when our flesh is in want, because—let's face it—our fleshly needs and desires drive much of our attention and focus. Teaching your flesh to turn to God while denying its most basic physiological need is a way of training your brain to turn to God in the midst of *any* need.

It is instilling the habit of focusing on God every time a need strikes. With every hunger pang, you are reminded *why* you are hungry, and it turns you toward Him.

*I need **You**, God. I need you more than food and everything this world tells me is essential. You are enough.*

When fasting, this cycle is repeated regularly. I see the leftover pizza in the fridge, and my stomach rumbles. I reach for it, then remember, "I'm fasting." There is a moment of decision. What do I want more? Each time I answer, "I want you more, God," and close the refrigerator door, a tiny bit of my flesh is chipped away.

It trains you to walk in the Spirit, for "the mind governed by the flesh is death, but the mind governed by the Spirit is life and peace."[330] If you want to be governed by the Spirit, you have to prepare your flesh to be OK when it doesn't get what it wants. If it never hears "no," your flesh will always throw a temper tantrum like a toddler when it is denied, and nine times out of ten, you'll give in.

But treating fasting only as training for the real world would be selling it short. It's so much more.

330 Romans 8:6

This habit of turning to God with every twinge of need also teaches you to pray without ceasing—an invaluable tool for staying in tune with the Holy Spirit.

People in the Bible fasted in mourning, in repentance, for God's guidance or protection, and simply to seek more of *Him*.

In Mark 9, after Jesus cast the demon out of the boy, the disciples ask why they could not "and He said unto them, 'This kind can come forth by nothing but by prayer and fasting.'"[331]

Fasting is a desperate outpouring of the spirit's need—whatever that need may be—and God does respond. In the Bible, fasting is often followed by a clear word from the Lord. It is pushing the world out and allowing the Lord in. It's a powerful way to teach yourself to mind the things of the spirit rather than the things of the flesh.[332]

Now that we've talked about what fasting is and what it's for, let's talk about what it *isn't*.

1) Fasting isn't a magic wand you can wave to receive God's favor, guidance, or forgiveness in lieu of actual dedication to Him and repentance.

Fasting requires an attitude of submission and a desire to do the Lord's will. Isaiah 58 is an especially harsh rebuke to those who fast but continue in their wicked ways—seeking their own pleasure, oppressing their workers, quarreling and fighting. God says He would rather have the fasting of obedience—that we loose the bonds of the oppressed, share our bread with the hungry, house the homeless, and clothe the naked. Fasting when you have no real desire for God or His precepts is simply posturing. And posturing before an omniscient God is one of the silliest, most

---

331 Mark 9:29 KJV
332 Romans 8:5

useless things you can do. God sees through to the intentions of our hearts and is not fooled by our actions. This is both comforting and terrifying, isn't it?

2) Fasting is not a thing you do to show what a wonderful Christian you are.

In Matthew 6:16, it says that no one who fasts so others will see and acknowledge their dedication will receive anything from the Lord, because they already have their reward—the approval of man. Let us never seek to do righteous acts for the attention it will afford us.

3) Fasting is not a form of self-harm meant to punish yourself.

Yes, it is for mourning and repentance, but even then, its purpose is to draw you closer to the Lord in spirit and away from the flesh. The Bible never speaks of it as a form of punishment, but an expression of grief and time to seek the Lord in earnest.

Lest I leave you with the idea I'm uber-spiritual, I also like using the word "practice" for fasting because I'm pretty terrible at it. But, as I say of all things you practice, you're always bad at something before you're good at it. Like an instrument, I'm sort of just making noise with it right now. I don't practice enough, so every time I pick it up, it feels rusty and unnatural. But eventually that noise will become smooth, musical, and it will begin to benefit not only me, but those around me with the beauty of its discipline and what it's doing in my soul.

Fasting can be a beautiful habit to develop to teach yourself to grow closer to the Lord, but it's also a tool we've been given to seek Him in times of distress and repent when our spirits are heavy with conviction. It is a tangible way to "turn to the Lord, so the veil is removed."[333]

TAKEAWAYS:

- Fasting is the practice of retraining your brain to turn to God instead of your own strength or worldly means when in need.
- Fasting is turning your heart from the fleshly to the spiritual, and emphasizes the fact that the eternal is more important than the worldly.
- Fasting also helps you to learn to "pray without ceasing." Each twinge of hunger causes your mind to be continually brought back to God.
- Any time your need is overwhelming, whether it be in grief or repentance or fear, fasting will help you draw closer to the Lord.
- Do not use fasting as a quick-fix magic ritual ensuring God will give you what you want, a display of your goodness, or a punishment. None of these are biblical.
- DO use fasting in order to seek more and more of the Lord in your life. Fasting is often followed by clear direction from the Holy Spirit.

---

333   2 Corinthians 3:16

SATISFACTION

Man finds it hard to get what he wants, because he does not want the best; God finds it hard to give, because He would give the best, and man will not take it.

George MacDonald

How do we learn to be satisfied in Christ, to abide in His rest and His peace, and to live free of the endless scrabbling, clawing, angst-ridden pursuit most of humanity seems to cycle through?

The answer to that question is long and complex and full of mystery, but it's also short and simple, and a child can understand it.

Make Christ your ultimate—no—your *only* aim. If we are spiritually hungry and thirsty and seeking satisfaction anywhere but in God, we will not experience the abundant life He wants to give. Jesus said, "I am the Bread of Life. Whoever comes to Me will never go hungry, and whoever believes in Me will never be thirsty."[334]

He is our hope, our future, our salvation, our water, and our bread. Too often, we starve our spirits by eating food that does not fill then cry out, "God, are you there? Do you even care?"

[334] John 6:35

But He's been there all along. We have received the invitation to His banquet, but we don't really believe the food He provides can replace what we already have. Like the men who gave excuses in the "Parable of the Great Banquet,"[335] when God calls, whatever we have going on feels too consequential to let go and take part in what He has for us.

And to attend the banquet *requires* a letting go. God has provisioned the table and supplied all our needs.[336] We must stop trusting our soul's sustenance to the things that will fade away and disappoint. I think we often try to attend God's banquet but continue nibbling stale food from our satchels when we think no one is looking.

We haven't "tasted and seen that the Lord is good,"[337] and we're afraid if we stop getting the nourishment we've chosen for ourselves, we will end up starving.

But doing this leaves us wondering why accepting God's invitation did not sustain—why it didn't "work."

I came to the table, God, but I'm still hungry.

S.D. Gordon recounts the story of a young man who planned to climb Mont Blanc. He was loaded down with items he insisted were essential, and no amount of protesting from the guide could convince him otherwise. Along the way, the young man slowly released every bit of his burden, realizing he could never reach the top while carrying it.

Gordon makes this comparison: "Many of us, when we find we can't reach the top with our loads, let the top go, and pitch our tents in the plain, and settle down with our small plans and accessories. The plain seems to be quite full of tents."

---

335   Luke 14:12-24
336   Philippians 4:19
337   Psalm 34:8

How many of us never learn to lay our burdens down and, instead, attempt to settle happily in the valley when God wants to take us to the splendor at the top of the mountain?

The man in the story, at least, came to realize the things he considered to be essentials were holding him back, but only after he'd become weary and worn with burdened climbing. If he had followed the guide's instructions from the start, how much easier his journey would have been!

If you cease putting your contentment in the things of this world, you'll find the journey far easier than if you wrestle them halfway up the mountain before submitting to your Guide's direction.

But we rarely cease our earthly strivings long enough to find out that God is really the cure for our soul's languor. As G.K. Chesterton said in *What's Wrong with the World*, "The Christian ideal has not been tried and found wanting. It has been found difficult and left untried."

We are like lame men who have been offered healing but will not release our crutches for fear of falling down. We can't wrap our heads around the fact that the crutches—money or power or relationships—will never make us whole—and indeed are holding us back. We stand at the foot of the mountain where we can see the steep cliffs and the scorched places above us and wonder how we will ever climb without everything we've relied on and enjoyed so far.

Many of the things we take for our sustenance may be good gifts from God's own hand; the problem comes when we begin to rely on them as we should only rely on God Himself. Everything else will pass away; our days are like grass that will wither in a moment.[338] "But godliness with contentment is great gain, for we

---

338   Psalm 103:15

brought nothing into the world, and we cannot take anything out of the world."[339]

Until we drop the crutches, we are actually hobbling our walk with God and making the climb that much more difficult. We must recognize the fleeting nature of all this world can provide and stop seeking satisfaction in the counterfeits rather than the real thing.

Bottom line—if you want your burden to be light, you've got to put some stuff down—everything, in fact, except God Himself. He will supply everything you need along the way.[340] And in seeking Christ alone, not only will your own thirst be quenched, the overflow will bless those around you. As John Piper says, "God is most glorified in us when we are most satisfied in Him."

Your source will be unlimited, so you will no longer be afraid of what you may lose. "Out of your heart will flow rivers of living water."[341]

I am finding this to be true of myself, especially in the area of time. I will admit to being quite stingy with my time. I have a lot of plans and projects and hobbies, and I literally never get bored. I could be at my house and not run out of things to do for years with only the ideas floating around in my head right now. In addition, I'm a super-introvert, so two hours given for someone else's need may mean another hour or more of decompressing before I have the headspace to write. So, I have grasped my time tightly in my own hands, unwilling to trust that God will spend it as I like if I let Him have it.

But God is reminding me that "my times are in *His* hands."[342] Holding onto my own agenda when He invites me to His ta-

---

339 I Timothy 6:6-7
340 Luke 12:24
341 John 7:37
342 Psalm 31:15

ble will never lead me to more satisfaction even if it might mean I complete more of my projects. Those are not the things that will fulfill me. I have no way of knowing which projects will ever amount to anything meaningful. But giving my time to God and allowing it to be spent as He sees fit will always yield the greatest good. As long as I am not wasting time being distracted, I can trust that His purposes will be accomplished in me. I can give of my time freely, unbegrudgingly (I'm still working on this), and without the fear of what I may not accomplish.

It is satisfaction in Christ alone and contentment regardless of your worldly circumstances that will allow you to live sacrificially. Indeed, it's difficult to take from someone living this way, because they hold loosely everything God has given them. No one took Christ's life from Him because He laid it down of His own accord.[343]

God is your source, and if you are believing Him with the kind of belief that results in obedience, "He will continually guide you and satisfy your desire in the scorched places."[344] At God's table, you will find His steadfast love,[345] and He will bring life to your soul.

"Come," God says, "everyone who thirsts, come to the waters; and he who has no money, come, buy and eat! Come, buy wine and milk without money and without price. Why do you spend your money for that which is not bread, and your labor for that which does not satisfy? Listen diligently to Me, and eat what is good, and delight yourselves in rich food. Incline your ear, and come to Me; hear, that your soul may live…."[346]

---

343 John 10:18
344 Isaiah 58:11
345 Psalm 136
346 Isaiah 55:1-3

When you feel spiritually empty, ask yourself if you've pitched your tent at the base of the mountain and refused the invitation to the Lord's banquet or if you've come to the table but continued seeking fulfillment in the things of this world.

Are you studying, learning, and meditating on His word? Are you worshipping and being intentionally thankful? Are you praying without ceasing and seeking the Kingdom of God first or have other things gotten in the way? Have you submitted to the Lord's will and ceased trusting in the fragile things of this world?

If we truly believe Jesus is the Bread of Life and the Living Water that will sate every hunger and slake every thirst, we will come to Him at the first pang of spiritual rumblings. We will not first feverishly immerse ourselves in our work or try a glass of wine or chocolate pie or our favorite TV show or go shopping or engage in a series of questionable relationships or scroll social media.

Jesus says, "Do not work for food that spoils, but for food that endures to eternal life, which the Son of Man will give you."[347]

If we have the Bread that will never spoil, but continue eating that which is perishable, our souls will starve while yet sitting at the banquet table.

Notice that Jesus tells us to work for the eternal food, and when the disciples asked *how* to do that, He answers thus: "This is the work of God, that you believe in Him whom He has sent."[348]

Once again, humanity asked for a blueprint, and God painted us a portrait—not a list of rules, but the person of Jesus Christ.

If a child of seven decided he wanted to show the ultimate love to his father and asked how to do it, he would probably expect (and even want) a list of things to do—taking out the trash every day or giving a prescribed number of hugs or keeping his room clean. But what the father really wants is for his son to grow

---

347 John 6:27
348 John 6:29

and change and learn from him every day. He wants them to have a relationship full of confidence so the son will always look to him and trust his advice. But explaining this to a seven-year-old will probably lead to confusion and possibly even disappointment. He wants to complete his duty of love and know without a doubt he's doing what's expected. But relationship doesn't work that way.

The father *may* want the son to take out the trash and give him hugs and keep his room clean, but if that's all that ever passes between them, the relationship will not be very satisfying for either one. It must expand and progress. What would please the father when the son is seven is hardly what would please him when the son is twenty.

The same is true of our heavenly Father. Our walk with Him should be constantly expanding and moving deeper into the understanding of who He is and a more confident dependence on His wisdom.

The belief that leads to eternal satisfaction requires that we be in relationship with Him. It's that belief we've talked about so much already—a belief that changes your life and affects your actions. It changes *you* and is always bringing you into richer understanding and truth. As the son will grow to understand his father better and better as he enters adulthood, we will begin to understand more and more of God as we mature in our faith. It's comforting to know that we don't have to wait to reach the summit of that mountain before our satisfaction begins to blossom. It is an ascent full of revelation and wonder about the Father Himself—the views become slowly more stunning and more expansive as we scale the mountain.

While others scramble to gain and worry over what they may lose in this life, may we be content in every situation—in want and in plenty, when hungry and fed, when brought low or living in abundance.[349] May we be satisfied in all circumstances, no matter how difficult, because "the Lord is our portion…therefore, we will hope in Him."[350]

If you want to immerse yourself in the contentment God promises, you must go to Him and Him alone for sustenance when your soul grows weak and weary. He does not mete out morsels to us sparingly. The banquet awaits.

TAKEAWAYS:
- Christ must be your only aim if you are to find the fulfillment He offers.
- If you keep eating the things of this world in search of satisfaction, you are not getting the sustenance your soul needs.
- If you want your burden to be light, you must put some things down. You cannot reach the peak of God's promise if you're carrying all the things this world says you need.
- Don't settle for the plains instead of the mountaintop. Trust God that His promises are true.
- When your soul feels empty, seek the things of God for its nourishment, not the things of this world.
- Seeking the things of God requires relationship; we cannot suddenly attain His heights. We must be in contact with our Guide and listening to His direction if we want our peace and rest in Him to grow.

---

349   Philippians 4:11
350   Lamentations 3:24

THANKFULNESS

It's one thing to be grateful. It's another to give thanks. Gratitude is what you feel. Thanksgiving is what you do.

Tim Keller

Our faith is like a fire, and fires need fuel. We want to build that fire to raging so that when the waves of doubt and fear and all the other obstacles come, they will not douse it.

This whole section is about some of the logs we can use to keep it blazing, and giving thanks is one powerful tool you can use. It is "proclaiming His wonderful deeds"[351] in order to remind yourself that "His steadfast love endures forever."[352] It is the act of remembering—indeed, of making it a *point* to remember—all that God has done for you in the past, so you can look forward and believe He will continue to take care of you in the future.

When the storms come, it's easy to listen to all the negative voices in your head like so many of the people we read about in the obstacles section:

Abraham: *He said He was going to make me a strong and mighty nation.*

---

351 Psalm 9:1
352 Psalm 136

The disciples in the storm: *Does He even care that we are perishing?*

Mary, Lazarus's sister: *If He had been here, Lazarus would not have died.*

But if we are drawing from a history with the Lord—if we have taken note of all the times He's provided for us, protected us, and fulfilled His promise—we can continue to warm ourselves by the fire of our faith. Without that fire, the storms will have us miserable and shivering in the wet and cold, thinking God has abandoned us.

Being thankful is something specific you can do to control your thoughts instead of letting your thoughts control you.

Martyn Lloyd-Jones says we should talk to ourselves instead of just listen—stand up to those negative voices in our heads and say, "Self, listen for a moment, I will speak to you" like David did in the Psalms: "Why are you cast down, O my soul, and why are you in turmoil within me? Hope in God; for I shall again praise Him."[353]

It seems unfathomable at the beginning of your faith journey, but we're actually told to "give thanks in all circumstances."[354] This becomes more and more possible the longer we've followed God's guidance and found Him faithful.

Corrie Ten Boom tells a story about when she was imprisoned with her sister Betsie in the concentration camp at Ravensbruck. They quickly realized their barracks were riddled with fleas, and Corrie cried, "Betsie, how can we live in such a place?"

Betsie began praying aloud and soon said she had the answer—they had read it just this morning from the Bible Corrie had smuggled in. The passage was I Thessalonians 5:14-18, which

---

353 Psalm 42:5
354 I Thessalonians 5:18

includes the verse we mentioned above: "...give thanks in all circumstances."

It took some time for Betsie to convince Corrie they should thank God for the fleas, but she eventually did so, still doubting that there could be any good reason for them.

Several weeks later, they learned that their barracks were left so unsupervised only *because of the fleas*. This had allowed them to continue reading the Bible to their fellow prisoners and bringing the hope of Christ to others, all because of their terrible circumstances.

Giving thanks is our declaration of faith even when the sentence is in, so to speak—when we're walking in the valley of the shadow of death, when we see no way out, and when we feel alone.

The Bible tells us those times will come. It also gives us example after example of people doing just that.

When Daniel found out he would be cast into a den of lions if he prayed to someone other than the king, he simply continued his normal habit of praying and giving thanks to God.[355]

The Lord closed the lion's mouths, and Daniel was spared.

When David was hiding in the caves as King Saul sought to kill him, David gave thanks and sang praises to God.[356]

God thwarted Saul's attempts to kill David, and he became king as was promised.

When Jesus told the disciples He was about to be delivered up and sacrificed, He was still giving thanks.[357]

Jesus's death came as He knew it would, but it was also reversed in His resurrection and was the fulfillment of God's promise to His children—a way for all of us to be reconciled to Him.

355 Daniel 6:10
356 Psalm 57:9
357 Matthew 26:2-27

We can rarely see what God is doing in dark valleys, the wanderings, and the hurts. When things seem like they can't get worse—when we're imprisoned in a flea-infested concentration camp, standing amongst the ravenous lions, hiding from our enemies in the cave, or someone has betrayed us—we need the habit of giving thanks to bring us hope.

I recommend pulling out those prayer cards we talked about. Keep track of the things you have prayed for—date them, even—so you have a written record of what you've asked and how God has answered. Do that for a few years, and I think you'll be surprised at how many have been undeniably answered by God's intervention.

You will have objective evidence that God answers prayer, and this will be faith-building not only for you, but also for others as you tell of His faithfulness.

You will be able to endure because you remember all the times God has saved you from impossible situations or wrought good out of terrible circumstances.

But this will only help if you've been trusting Him along the way. You rarely need to be rescued from the shallows or the shore. If you've never "launched out into the deep at His word,"[358] you will never learn to be certain of Him, and when the riptide drags you out farther than you can swim, you will have little confidence that God can save you. You never built up any evidence that He could—or even that He wanted to.

Here, again, we see the necessity for an active faith—that *belief* we've already talked about so much. It is an essential predecessor to meaningful thanksgiving. Without specific instances of God's faithfulness in your own life, you will only be attempting to muster up the *feeling* of gratitude.

358   Luke 5:3-5

But feelings are not the fire of faith; neither are they its fuel. They're not even its heat. They are merely the smoke, and smoke is rarely the primary goal of a fire; it is a byproduct. Making the feeling your goal is futile—like trying to catch smoke in your hands—and when times are hard, that feeling will dissipate and leave you shivering in the cold. Seeking the smoke itself will have you fueling your fire with unseasoned logs; it may smoke and sputter a bit, but it will never blaze.

Smoke *does* have a purpose as we can see from the old adage, "Where there's smoke, there's fire." It sends up a signal that helps others see your faith and draws them to its source, but attempting to work up the smoke, i.e. draw others to Christ, without actually feeding the fire is pointless.

Even as others draw near, they will realize the smoke is not what they wanted, but the warmth of the salvation of God and a light by which they can see their way. Without that, the smoke is merely something that gets in your eyes, obscuring your vision. Feelings alone will never keep you on the path of God.

Real gratitude will arise naturally from real acts of trusting God, not from the mere idea of trusting Him or because you're fabricating a feeling without any basis for it.

We cannot take feelings as the main thing or as evidence of the main thing. If we do that, our faith will flare and fizzle just as they do, and if I am any indicator, my feelings are about as fickle as the weather and therefore as reliable as the weatherman.

I do not mean to make Christianity out as a kind of stoicism. Positive feelings are a gift from God, and we should enjoy them. And I think as we mature in our walk with Christ, those feelings of gratitude, love, peace, and all the rest will grow more and more constant, because the longer we walk with Him, the more they will be grounded in *His* constancy instead of the things of the world. But even then, we are not immune to despair in hard times or illness or exhaustion, and if our faith is dependent on the feeling, we will at least falter, if not fall.

I'm sure some of you are thinking our gratitude should be full already from the great sacrifice of Jesus alone. You would be right; it is the "pearl of great price,"[359] and God has given us more than we deserve in it.

And I'm convinced that as our faith matures and we grow to understand His sacrifice more deeply, that gratitude will become more and more all-encompassing.

But we are like children. And gratitude must grow as the child grows. He first learns gratitude as simple words to say for things given—gifts and food. At some point, the child becomes conscious of his father's love and realizes it is far more valuable than the things given. It is only much later when he is able to recognize how much his father sacrificed in instruction and time and work and resources.

From the first, the child is basking in the love and benefiting from the sacrifice, but he does not have the capacity to understand its depth until he is grown—or very nearly so. Once the grateful son sees that the father has already given all, he wants nothing more than the father's presence in his life—to enjoy him for who he is and all he's already done.

We are the same; we must progress in gratitude as we progress in our Christian walk. And like that child, we will eventually see the enormity of our Father's great sacrifice, and He alone will become an unlimited source of fuel for our faith.

Conventional psychology also recognizes that gratitude is a mindset that increases happiness. Taking the time to be intentionally grateful trains our brains to look for the good instead of the

---

359   Matthew 13:45-46

bad, and that doesn't come naturally. Many of us have "problem radar"—always seeking out the bad and focusing on it.

So, when you practice thankfulness, you're not only building a more solid faith, you're actually remapping your brain so seeing the positive becomes easier and more natural, leaving you happier and more content. In this world of thickets and thorns, a practice of thankfulness will have you looking for roses.

TAKEAWAYS:
- Thankfulness is the act of remembering the things God has done for you, and it will grow your faith, helping you trust Him more in the future.
- The act of being thankful is a way to control your thoughts instead of allowing them to control you.
- "Giving thanks in all things" is hard, but God can always work a beautiful purpose, even in the most difficult situation you've ever faced.
- Thankfulness will help fuel the fires of your faith in the dark and in the cold.
- Your thankfulness will also be a testament to others that God is faithful.
- Don't start by trying to muster up the feeling of being grateful; start with actually *believing* what God says. If you've never followed Him beyond your own abilities, you will not have much confidence that He can save you in the depths.
- The feeling of being grateful will come and go, but your faith can remain solid if you are resting on the things God has already done.
- Your gratitude will grow in depth as your faith matures.

DELIGHT

If you have no joy, there's a leak in your Christianity somewhere.

Billy Sunday

I only now begin to understand why God prompted the specific topics I've talked about in the "Preventative Measures" section. It seemed sort of a hodge-podge once I realized I'd come to the end—like I'd forgotten some (most) of the standard spiritual disciplines while also making up a few of my own.

But now I see it.

These are the topics I needed, so they're the ones He had me write about, and here we are at its culmination: delight.

I wasn't expecting it. I expected devotion and perseverance and a wealth of other respectable virtues, but delight didn't even cross my mind. God wants those other things, to be sure—my belief and hope and fasting and satisfaction and thankfulness and prayer—but He also wants my *delight*.

The Bible tells us over and over to delight and rejoice in the Lord. Funny how we never seem to realize that means we will be delighted or that we will feel like rejoicing.

God impressed this on my mind a few months ago, and I realized I wasn't very good at delighting, so I started mulling it over.

Maybe because it's easier to undertake, God had me start with remembering how to delight in *things* first.

And I say remembering, because I certainly used to know how. But delight withers if we don't water it, and why is that?

Because delight takes time; it takes paying attention—really seeing a thing instead of taking it for granted and genuinely engaging in an activity instead of rushing through it.

Because how can you enjoy anything if your mind is already on to the next thing?

When I delight in nature, I hear the crickets' chorus, feel the breeze on my face, smell the petrichor after the rain, observe how the crape myrtle bends its boughs to the bloom, and catch a glimpse of the iridescent hummingbird hovering like a fairy.

Delighting takes time. We did not begrudge this when we were children. We felt we had all the time in the world. A child may spend an hour searching for a rock with just the right shape or a day hunting a four-leafed clover or a week creating a fort in the woods.

When I started my journey into delight, I forced myself to stop rushing through things, but to pay attention, to discover, and to savor what there was to delight in even if it wasn't as beautiful as the nature scene I described above.

Cooking was an area in which I attempted to inject delight. It was a thing I'd been rushing through, treating it only as a bother, and the results made that apparent. The food was edible, but uninspiring. There was no neglect of duty, but I was only completing a task, not being attentive to that task and taking time with it.

So I tried to change that. Instead of attempting to cook the fastest, easiest thing I could think of, I started considering what I might actually like to make and what my husband might actually like to eat. It made me more creative. It resulted in better food and a husband who was also now delighted! Ironically, it made me *less* frustrated with the chore, though I was spending more time doing it.

If we transfer that experience to spiritual life, could it be that we have little delight in it because we've turned it all into duty? Are we rushing through those duties as things to be done and crossed off the list instead of activities to be savored because they create richness and depth and satisfaction in our lives? As I savored the act of cooking, the food became not only more flavorful, but more nourishing.

We don't delight in anything when we see it only as a problem to be solved.

Tending our garden is not a delight if we're only ever doing it so the yard looks right and no one thinks ill of us. It becomes a delight when we are doing the yard work so we can sit in the garden and walk among the flowers.

Minding our children is not a delight if we're only ever interested in feeding and clothing them and making sure they act right. It becomes a delight when we engage with them, watch them play, and take the time to know them as human beings in their own right.

Could it be that so many Christians' lives grow cold and joyless because they are participating in the duty, but have never even attempted the delight? The duty seems burdensome and difficult if you never move beyond it.

No relationship is complete if all is duty. I've realized that even my cats relish being delighted in. There are times they seem to want nothing—not to be petted or have a snack or a toy—but if I stop looking at them or walk away, they become dissatisfied all the same. Children, too, can tell if someone is attentive only out of obligation. It's the time and attention spent with no agenda that allows love to grow full. As with a spouse, the duties of marriage are important and without them the love would likely grow cold, but the relationship deepens with the long talks and the intentional date nights—the time set apart simply for delighting in each other.

The Bible says that the joy of the Lord is our strength.[360] This makes sense as you apply it to other things as well. If we find no joy in our marriages, they will become fragile. If we find no joy in our children, we will neglect them and both they and the relationship will grow weak. When I found no joy in cooking, the meals definitely could not have been described as strong.

Finding joy in the Lord is the surest way to build a strong faith, because you will have learned the beauty of Him and come to understand what would be lost if you drifted. It is also the surest way to draw others to Him. No one will be drawn to God through your bitterness, cynicism, resignation, or drudgery.

And notice that cooking and yardwork and rearing children are not one-time, fix-it-and-forget-it moments. I cooked, but I must keep cooking. I tend my yard, but I will have to weed again. If I correct a child once, I have not finished teaching him.

The duty must be repeated regularly with a focus on the inherent worth of *now*, and the joy the duty will bring. This attentive, intentional participation will grow the duty into strong delight that deepens over time. The pinnacle of delight is not reached at the wedding, but in the marriage; not at the birth, but throughout the childhood; and not at the moment of salvation, but in the process of sanctification.

Delight is not divorced from duty. As with the other things I've mentioned, the path to delight begins with an action of obedience. The feeling rarely comes first.

360 Nehemiah 8:10

I could not delight in cooking if I stopped doing it. You cannot delight in your child—not for very long anyway—if you stop giving him instruction. A marriage would not be very delightful if the partners ceased to do their duty by it.

But when delight is in full bloom, the duty itself is transformed into a delight. David says, "I delight to do your will, O my God; your law is within my heart."[361]

My attempt to delight in cooking became a way of delighting in my husband, and seeing *his* delight made the duty itself a joy.

In the same way, as we learn to pay attention to the spiritual disciplines—not to rush through them as chores or interruptions—we delight the Lord, and when we begin to feel that delight through stronger and stronger promptings of the Holy Spirit, the duties no longer seem a burden, but something to look forward to.

It was through the duties that the Lord guided me to delight, because I was spending the time to pay attention to Him. As I drew near to Him, He drew near to me.[362] We are able to delight in the Lord not in the absence of duty, but through savoring it.

I'm afraid we've very much lost delight, joy, and rejoicing as earmarks of the Christian faith. Let's change that.

Let us, like children, seek Him as the child seeks the rock and the four-leafed-clover, as if we have all the time in the world. And why shouldn't we? God is not bound by time. If He wants us to delight in Him, and He's aware of the time it takes, who are we to question?

Even in the writing of this chapter, I stuttered through several very unoriginal beginnings over several days and grew frazzled and fearful I wouldn't meet my self-imposed deadline. Then I heard that little whisper:

361 Psalm 40:8
362 James 4:8

Stop. Go outside. Don't just write about delight; go be delighted!

As I obeyed, the direction became clear: "The heavens declare the glory of God, and the sky above proclaims His handiwork."[363]

God didn't have me learning to delight in things first because it was easier, but because He made delightful things for me to enjoy, and when I enjoy them, they direct me to delight in Him.

I made a delightful dinner for my husband to enjoy, but he did not praise the dinner for being good; he praised me for making it.

Delighting in the Lord is more than an item to cross off your list; it's a plant you water, a marriage you cultivate, and a child you rear—and you do so because you love the plant and your spouse and your child and want to see them thrive in the same way you want your relationship with the Lord to thrive.

You may stumble upon some joys in any of these situations even while ponderously doing your duty or rushing to get to the next thing, and you may experience some moments of joy in Christ without taking the time to revel in Him. But you would miss more.

I feel I've only cracked the door on delighting in the Lord, allowing the tiniest sliver to warm my face. Yet, it's awakened my soul to the sun that must await once the door is flung full open—a delight so strong and brilliant I will have to close my eyes to bask in it.

---

[363] Psalm 19:1

TAKEAWAYS:
- God doesn't only want your duty; He wants your delight.
- Delight only grows when we are paying attention; it will not come when you are rushing through your chores or prayers or Bible reading in order to cross them off your list.
- Delight grows fuller over time and with intention.
- Through delighting, the duties themselves become delights.
- Delighting in the things around you and your daily tasks leads to delight in God, for "through Him all things were made."[364]

---

[364] John 1:3

THINGS UNSEEN

All their life in this world and all their adventures had only been the cover and the title page. Now, at last, they were beginning Chapter One of the Great Story which no one on earth has read, which goes on forever, in which every chapter is better than the one before.[365]

C.S. Lewis, *The Last Battle*

The other night I had a bad dream. It wasn't a nightmare—just a series of difficult, unpleasant, and uncomfortable tasks. It seemed really important that I get them done, but I couldn't keep up, and things kept going wrong. When I woke up, there was a lingering moment of stress and anxiety before I realized...*it was just a dream!*

Ahh, the relief!

I have a feeling something similar will happen when I slip from this world into the next. My mind will be all aflutter with troubles and worries until the moment I open my eyes and see Jesus.

[365] *The Last Battle* by C.S. Lewis © Copyright C.S. Lewis Pte Ltd 1956. Extract reprinted by permission.

Then all that anxiety will fall away. I'll realize that most of the silly little things I fussed and fretted over mattered no more than that dream. And even of the important things, I'll wonder how I never understood that God's glory, faithfulness, power, and sovereignty covered all.

"For now, we see in a mirror dimly, but then face to face. Now I know in part; then I shall know fully, even as I have been fully known."[366]

I am fully known, and one day I will also know in full. I will grasp that He is Abba, Father. And good fathers, even earthly ones, run to their children when they cry out in the night. They comfort and protect the child even when the monsters aren't real. Our Father is holding us every time we tremble in fear, even at the things that don't matter.

But we don't *have* to tremble. We can learn to trust God's promises and who He is and walk with Him. We can skip all that pesky fear and uncertainty, because our lives are like a breath, and our days are like a passing shadow[367]—"only the cover and title page," as Lewis states in the opening quote.

We will realize how fleeting this world is and marvel at how much time we wasted on the passing troubles of earth.

I don't plan on waiting. I want to live for the things that matter. I want to "look not to the things that are seen but to the things that are unseen. For the things that are seen are transient, but the things that are unseen are eternal."[368] I am determined to look at the *real* things—the eternal things—not the dream.

When I started this book, I had in my mind to call it something like *"Tangibles: The Things that Distract us from God,"* or *"Intangibles: The Things that Really Matter."* I decided the title needed

366   I Corinthians 13:12
367   Psalm 144:4
368   2 Corinthians 4:18

to be broadened, but the essence of the *seen* vs. the *unseen* has still driven the entire work.

If I had to sum up everything I've written, it would be this: focus on the eternal, not the temporal. Seek ye first the Kingdom of God….

It sounds simplistic and trite, but that's only because we've heard it so many times. The unseen world encompasses everything that matters—love and kindness and hope and all the fruits of the Spirit. It is God's presence and infinity with Him.

There are so many verses that encourage us to continue to follow God *now* in light of the glory we will have with Him in eternity.

"No eye has seen, nor ear heard, nor the heart of man imagined, what God has prepared for those who love him."[369]

"And let us not grow weary of doing good, for in due season we will reap, if we do not give up."[370]

"When the perishable puts on the imperishable, and the mortal puts on immortality, then shall come to pass the saying that is written: 'Death is swallowed up in victory. O death, where is your victory? O death, where is your sting?'…Therefore, my beloved brothers, be steadfast, immovable, always abounding in the work of the Lord, knowing that in the Lord your labor is not in vain."[371]

When the perishable puts on the imperishable, and the mortal puts on immortality….

In other words, when the unseen becomes more real than the seen.

By faith, Moses "endured as seeing Him who is invisible."[372]

---

369 2 Corinthians 2:9
370 Galatians 6:9
371 I Corinthians 15:54-55, 58
372 Hebrews 11:27

All of the believers in the Hebrews 11 Faith Chapter "died in faith, not having received the things promised, but having seen them and greeted them from afar, and having acknowledged that they were strangers and exiles on the earth. For people who speak thus make it clear that they are seeking a homeland. If they had been thinking of that land from which they had gone out, they would have had opportunity to return. But as it is, they desire a better country, that is, a heavenly one."[373]

They knew the best this world has to offer isn't worth striving for compared to the better country—the heavenly one. They lived as if they could see it, though they could not.

All we can see will pass away—our homes, our money, our work, our lives, and the lives of all those we love—all of it is transient. "All flesh is like grass and all its glory like the flower of grass. The grass withers, and the flower falls, but the word of the Lord remains forever."[374]

God's promises stand stronger than all the *stuff* we can see around us. *Believing God* as Abraham did will lead us into a beautiful, peaceful relationship with our Lord, firmly fixed in confidence and hope regardless of the difficulty and pain in the world around us.

The things of the world shout for your attention—they beckon, they tempt, and they promise. But if you look at your efforts to satisfy your soul so far—and if you're honest—you can see that filling yourself to the brim with things you can taste and touch and see *isn't working*. Your soul is still hungry, your spirit still unfulfilled. Maybe it's time to try something different—to fix your eyes on the "inheritance that is imperishable, undefiled, and unfading, kept in Heaven for you."[375]

[373] Hebrews 11:13-16
[374] I Peter 1:24-25
[375] I Peter 1:4

The man who sets his sights on the Kingdom of God is always moving toward his goal in eternity; the man who sets his sights on the things of this earth is always moving away from them toward death[376]—"our outer self is wasting away, our inner self is being renewed day by day."[377]

I am striving to live that way—to "set my mind on things that are above, not on things that are on earth,"[378] to follow where the Lord leads even when I don't understand it, to trust He is working all things for good even when I don't like it, to believe He can bring the impossible to pass, to look forward to the city with foundations whose designer and builder is God,[379] and to rest in His promises even when the world around me is descending into chaos and instability.

We need not fear that chaos or instability, "for we know that if the tent that is our earthly home is destroyed, we have a building from God, a house not made with hands, eternal in the heavens."[380]

While I can't recommend this show carte blanche, the episode "Tapestry" of *Daredevil* stated it perfectly: "God's plan is like a beautiful tapestry and the tragedy of being human is that we only get to see it from the back—ragged threads and muddy colors—we only get a hint of the beauty that would be revealed if we could see the whole pattern on the other side."

While this is true, it doesn't have to be a tragedy. We can have a faith that is the assurance of things hoped for, the conviction of things not seen.[381]

---

376 An idea for which I'm almost certain I owe some writer credit, but I can't remember who that person is.
377 I Corinthians 4:16
378 Colossians 3:2
379 Hebrews 11:10
380 2 Corinthians 5:1
381 Hebrews 11:1

My prayer is that you would begin to trust His weavings—to walk by faith and not by sight.[382] It's sort of ironic that walking by sight seems to have us blundering about in every direction attempting to find our way, while walking by faith has only one path—the path to Christ.

"Therefore, let us run with endurance the race that is set before us, looking to Jesus, the founder and perfecter of our faith, who for the joy that was set before Him endured the cross, despising the shame, and is seated at the right hand of the throne of God. Consider Him who endured from sinners such hostility against Himself, so that you may not grow weary or fainthearted."[383]

The joy set before us is worth it. God has "put eternity into our hearts,"[384] though we are too small to comprehend His plan from beginning to end. Our meager threads are too short for us to see the pattern in the grand tapestry, but He has told of it, and we can see its truth in story after story as we read the Word.

With each thread and each stitch, whether shadow or light, He is weaving, in you, a great and beautiful story.

---

382   2 Corinthians 5:7
383   Hebrews 12:1-3
384   Ecclesiastes 3:11

www.ingramcontent.com/pod-product-compliance
Lightning Source LLC
Chambersburg PA
CBHW071341080526
44587CB00017B/2912